About the author

Ambreena Manji is a Reader in the
Department of Law, University of Keele. Prior
to that, she taught law and development at the
School of Law, University of Warwick. She is
also a Fellow of the Institute of Commonwealth
Studies, University of London. She has written extensively on land reform, gender and
development, and the role of international
financial institutions.

AMBREENA MANJI

The politics of land reform in Africa

From communal tenure to free markets

Zed Books
LONDON | NEW YORK

The politics of land reform in Africa: from communal tenure to free markets was first published in 2006 by Zed Books Ltd, 7 Cynthia Street, London N1 9JF, UK and Room 400, 175 Fifth Avenue, New York, NY 10010, USA.

<www.zedbooks.co.uk>

Copyright © Ambreena Manji, 2006

The right of Ambreena Manji to be identified as the author of this work has been asserted by her in accordance with the Copyright, Designs and Patents Act, 1988.

Cover designed by Andrew Corbett
Set in Arnhem and Futura Bold by Ewan Smith, London
Index: <ed.emery@britishlibrary.net>

A catalogue record for this book is available from the British Library.
US CIP data are available from the Library of Congress.

ISBN 1 84277 494 8 | 978 1 84277 494 6 hb
ISBN 1 84277 495 6 | 978 1 84277 495 3 pb

Contents

Acknowledgements

I have benefited from discussing the ideas contained in this book at seminars at the Council for the Development of Social Science Research in Africa, Dakar; the International Institute for the Sociology of Law, Onati; the Centre for Socio-Legal Studies, Wolfson College, Oxford; the Centre for African Studies, Cambridge; the Institute of Commonwealth Studies, University of London; Emory Law School, Atlanta; Stanford Law School, California; the School of Law, Trinity College, Dublin; the School of Law, Queen's University, Belfast; Kent Law School; and the School of Law, Birkbeck College. I am grateful to the participants on these occasions for their comments and encouragement.

I gratefully acknowledge the support of my colleagues at Keele Law School and thank my students at Melbourne, Warwick and Keele for their interest in the topic of African land reform. At Zed, I am grateful for the enthusiasm and assistance of Robert Molteno and Ellen McKinlay. Finally, my thanks to John Harrington for his invaluable help and support.

1 Introduction

The politics of land reform in Africa

In many parts of Africa, the last two decades have been characterized by debates as to the purpose and direction of land reform, the appointment of commissions of inquiry into land matters, the formulation of national land policies and ultimately by the enactment of new land laws. In short, this has been the age not just of land reform but of land law reform. We have reached an important historical juncture: many countries – among them Eritrea, Ethiopia, Rwanda, Tanzania, Uganda, Malawi, Zambia, Mozambique, South Africa and Namibia – are now considering the implications of the new legislative changes in land relations with which they are faced. The main thrust of the new legislation is to liberalize land tenure and to facilitate the creation of markets in land.

My aim in this book is to explore the politics of land reform in Africa and, in particular, to understand the recent revival of interest in the role of law to bring about development. I seek to identify the elements of a network of African land law reform and to explore the ways in which the network is created and sustained. This network is made up of significant groups whose interests are translated into issues of land law reform. As I show, international financial institutions such as the World Bank, international donors such as the British Department for International Development, African governments, legislators, non-governmental organizations, legal consultants, commercial lenders and the judiciary have all been important actors over the past two decades. Their concerns have been translated into issues of land law reform.

Altering land relations

In his address to the British Labour Party in 2002, former US President Bill Clinton gave the following account of a recent African tour:

> I have just come here from a trip to Africa which provided me with all kinds of fresh evidence of the importance of politics ... In Ghana ... a new President is working with a great Peruvian economist, Hernando de Soto, to bring the assets of poor people in to the legal system so they can be collateral for loans.[1]

His comments are a reminder that, out of office, Clinton remains committed to the neo-liberal agenda pursued by his administration, as evidenced by the coming into being of the North American Free Trade Agreement and the establishment of the World Trade Organization.[2] As 'World President of the Third Way'[3] his words were designed to convey his commitment to inclusion: as long as poor people remain outside the legal system they are not able to participate in the free market. The thrust of Clinton's words was that although Ghana's citizens are poor they might be brought with some guidance to perceive their only asset, their land, as good collateral for loans. Indeed, he has described de Soto's work as 'the most promising anti-poverty initiative in the world'.[4]

De Soto's project, as elaborated in his enticingly entitled book, *The Mystery of Capital: Why Capitalism Triumphs in the West and Fails Everywhere Else*,[5] has met with considerable interest from international financial institutions and bilateral donors. For this reason, it is important to set out the main contours of de Soto's argument here. According to de Soto, it is the lack of formalized property rights which explains the failure of non-western countries (the 'everywhere else' of the book's subtitle) to develop. It is not that the poor do not have assets. Indeed, we are told that 'the entrepreneurial ingenuity of the poor has created wealth on a vast scale'.[6] The problem, however, is that 'they hold these resources in defective forms'.[7] To take one example: 'houses built on land whose ownership rights are not adequately recorded'.[8]

The solution advocated by de Soto reserves a central role for the law. His programme advocates legal solutions which entail bringing what are described as the assets of the poor into the legal system. This would entail submitting to the process of 'representation', to the process, that is, of registration and titling. When land, for example, is 'represented in a property document',[9] it is enabled to lead 'a parallel life alongside [its] material existence. [It] can be used as collateral for loans.'[10] This is the cause of wealth in 'the West'[11] where there is 'an implicit legal infrastructure hidden deep within their property systems – of which ownership is but the tip of the iceberg. The rest of the iceberg is an intricate man-made process that can transform assets and labour into capital.'[12]

De Soto argues that research conducted by his Institute for Liberty and Democracy has estimated that the poor in developing countries own some 9.3 trillion dollars in assets to which they nevertheless do not have title. As a result, in confronting the problems of developing countries 'we shouldn't just focus on the macroeconomic side of the formula: stable money, fiscal equilibrium, and privatisation. The core of the capitalist system as I understand it, is that it is essentially a legal property system.'[13] For de Soto, 'law is the instrument that fixes and realises capital'.[14] The law plays a central role because 'assets need a formal property system to produce significant surplus value'.[15] De Soto's project is summed up in the observation that: 'It is the property system that draws out the abstract potential from buildings and fixes it in representations that allow us to go beyond passively using the buildings only as shelters.'[16] As I show below, de Soto's approach to land is echoed in recent documents of the World Bank in which land that is used 'merely as shelter' rather than a source of capital is similarly deprecated.[17]

De Soto's work has met with widespread approval among policy-makers as I show in Chapter 3. Clinton's endorsement of

3

his work was followed by high-level meetings in London between de Soto and members of the British government. His programme is thought to have had a considerable influence on thinking on land issues at the UK's Department for International Development.[18] It is also certain that other African countries will be studying de Soto's project in Ghana. To aid this process and in order to disseminate his ideas on the formalization of property rights, de Soto has created the Foundation for Building the Capital of the Poor in Accra. One of the stated objectives of the Foundation is 'to establish a regional training centre ... for the benefit of other countries interested in the property reform programme'.[19] Awareness of de Soto's project is spreading. The United Nations Development Programme (UNDP) has given its support to the quest to formalize land rights. Its resident representative in Ghana has sought to emphasize the broad political relevance of property rights, stating that they constitute a governance issue and that their acquisition can 'transform the ordinary folk into a potentially active economic agent, indeed a wealth creator ... we are talking about the direct link between governance and wealth creation and poverty reduction.'[20] Voicing his support for de Soto, Ghana's President Kufuor hailed the transformation of land into 'bankable property' which would give holders of land titles access to credit: 'this could prove the vital part of the missing link that might help generate the prosperity that we all yearn for.'[21]

By the time of Clinton's visit to Africa, the World Bank was already working on the process of reviewing its global involvement in lending in the land sector. I discuss the role of the World Bank in promoting land law reform in Chapter 3, but a brief summary of its outlook on land relations is provided here. The last review of land issues by the World Bank was carried out in 1975.[22] In 2001, it completed what it described as a 'lessons learned' study which formed the basis of an electronic consultation that year.[23] The following year, the World Bank issued two draft reports on land policy. These reports were projects of the

4

World Bank's Research Department with the collaboration of multilateral and bilateral organizations such as the Department for International Development (DfID); Germany's Gesellschaft für technische Zusammenarbeit (GTZ); and the United States' Agency for International Development (USAID). The draft reports were presented as the culmination of a two-year-long process of review by the Bank of its global involvement in lending in the land sector. As part of the World Bank's consultation process, it presented the first draft at four regional workshops. These workshops were promoted as opportunities to discuss the draft report with, and receive feedback from, civil society groups and other interested parties. The second draft of the report was then released by the World Bank which posted it on the internet and invited comments. It is on the basis of these two consultation periods that the Bank published the final policy research report, entitled *Land Policies for Growth and Poverty Reduction*, in 2003.[24]

Policy research reports are the most important vehicles which the Bank's researchers can employ to attempt to influence thinking on a particular issue from within the institution. They are generally produced at a rate of only one a year. It can therefore be expected that the final policy research report will be influential in setting the policy agenda over the coming years. However, the World Bank was severely criticized by a number of civil society groups for failing to consult to any meaningful extent on the draft reports. Criticisms which were levelled at the Bank included its reliance on a small number of experts, its failure to invite civil society groups to attend workshops, the exclusion of landless peoples, the failure to circulate the drafts to interested parties, an over-reliance on the internet and the imposition of severe timeframes on the process of consultation.[25] It is worthwhile to quote at length an open letter to the World Bank signed by a number of South African organizations which read:

We hereby express our profound concern about the land policies

5

of the World Bank generally, and in particular, about the current process through which future World Bank land policies are being defined. This process of redefinition will not only be decisive for the future land programmes of the World Bank, but will also have a strong impact on co-operation policies at bilateral and multilateral level and on national agrarian reform policies. According to the information we have received, the World Bank will be organising regional seminars on different continents over the coming months to undertake the formulation and drafting of a 'Land Policy Research Report' ... This document – which is expected to have a wide international impact – will later be redrafted by a small group of experts. The Bank has announced that the process of redefinition will be transparent and will include the participation and consultation of civil society, and the new policies which emerge from this process are supposed to be 'defined with the participation of civil society'. If the above is true, it begs a number of questions, beginning with the question of 'who defines 'civil society'? We further would like to know what mandate such 'civil society' would have to help define a policy that is expected to be carried out by governments? We further note the absence of landless and peasant organisations on the list of invited participants. We believe it is impossible to embark on a 'participatory' process to define land policies without including the peasants' perspective. The presence and role of the few civil society organisations appears to be very limited by the current process. The organisations involved run the risk of being used to legitimate the claim of a 'consultative' process to justify the World Bank policies. We are also concerned about the lack of clarity regarding the manner and extent to which the seminars will influence the final product ... to be drafted by a few experts – in fundamental contradiction to the supposed participatory approach. Finally, even less clarity exists regarding this document's influence on the actual policies of the World Bank.[26]

According to the final policy research report published in 2003, land does more than simply provide a shelter and a means of livelihood. It is also to be understood as 'a main vehicle for investing, accumulating wealth, and transferring it between generations'.[27] Access to land affects incentives to make investments and the ability of the poor to access financial markets. Thus, for the World Bank, land is fundamental not just to poverty reduction but to economic growth. Policies that make it possible to use land as a means to access credit turn it into an economically viable resource resulting in what the Bank terms 'equity benefits'.[28] The ability of households to access credit using their land as collateral has widespread implications on two levels according to the World Bank. First, it affects the household's ability to make indivisible investments and, second, it affects the emergence and working of rural credit markets.[29] From this perspective, economic growth as a whole is held back if the assets of the poor are allowed to remain outside the system of formal credit.

The acquisition of secure tenure rights not only increases investment in land, for example in the form of labour inputs, it is also seen as increasing the supply of credit from formal credit institutions using land as collateral. Although it admits the empirical evidence to support it is scant, the Bank believes that the ability to use land as collateral for raising credit and the existence of a well developed land sales market could enhance social mobility.[30] The emergence of financial markets to parallel and support markets in land is seen as having a beneficial impact on the broader rural economy by raising funds for both agricultural and non-agricultural activities, by providing working capital and by enabling access to credit as insurance. Incomplete credit markets are thus seen as imperfections in wider markets.[31]

This approach to land has been summed up in the characteristically succinct words of *The Economist* as follows:

Africans find it hard to use what they have to best advantage

7

because they lack secure property rights. Very few can prove that they own their land or their homes, because they do not have title deeds. This matters, because without a reliable system for ascertaining who owns what, assets cannot be used as collateral. In rich countries, if a farmer wants to invest in better seeds or bigger tractors, he can probably borrow the necessary cash using his land as security. If he fails to honour his debt, the bank takes the land. If all does well, however, his easy access to credit allows him to make his land more productive, which in turn increases its worth. Asset-backed lending is a crucial element in the dynamism of advanced capitalist countries. In America, for example, the most common way for an entrepreneur to raise start-up capital is by mortgaging the family home.[32]

Transparently taking its cue from the recently published World Bank global land policy, *The Economist* argues that the future lies in a transition from peasant subsistence to petty bourgeois entrepreneurship. The Bank's overall advocacy of rural credit markets is summed up in the suggestion that without them 'poor people would fail to get out of poverty not because they are unproductive or lack skills, but because, due to credit market imperfections, they never get the opportunity to utilise their innate ability'.[33]

Land Policies for Growth and Poverty Reduction is richly suggestive. It brings religious imagery to the business of economics. Land which is unused (or unusable) because it has not been brought into the legal system by registration and titling is described as a dead asset. Africa's entrepreneurial spirit and the innate ability of poor people will only flourish with the liberation of dead capital. The influence of de Soto on the World Bank's thinking is clear: in both its language and its substantive content the report draws on de Soto's work.

It should not surprise us to find that Clinton's support for the formalization of land rights as a means to access credit – which was articulated in the language of poverty reduction to the British Labour Party Conference – is accurately reflected in the World Bank's global land policy document. As Callinicos has pointed out, there is a close relationship between the promotion of neo-liberal economic programmes by US governments and by international financial institutions.

> At the global level, the imposition of neo-liberal orthodoxy at least in part reflected a conscious strategy pursued by successful American administrations in order to maintain US hegemony in the post-Cold War era: the very name attached to these policies – the Washington Consensus – is symptomatic of the role played in their implementation by the institutional complex binding together the US treasury, the IMF, and the World Bank.[34]

Now linked with underdevelopment, non-formalized property relations must be discouraged. However, in an evolutionary mode of thinking[35] the World Bank concedes this need not be done all at once: in relation to land, those areas which are most productive or valuable should be given priority.[36] The formalization of property rights has none the less become a central component of development policy, giving the law an important role in development. This idea is taken up in Chapter 3.

The revival of 'law and development'

The contemporary interest in using law to bring about development is not new. It has historical roots in the immediate post-independence period. As an area of scholarship and practice, 'law and development' can be traced to the late 1960s.[37] At that time, the main concern of law and development scholars and practitioners was to provide technical assistance to government ministries and to boost their administrative efficiency in order to bring about development. The law and development movement had a pragmatic and instrumentalist view of the role of law.[38] Lawyers played a central role in what Samir Amin has characterized as a 'bourgeois national project' of developmentalism[39] but by the

9

mid-1970s, it seemed that both as an area of scholarship and as a policy-oriented practice the methods, outlook and objectives of law and development had been abandoned.[40]

Today, law and development scholarship and practice are widely held to have been reborn[41] as economic globalization witnesses a 'market-oriented development model'[42] imposed on peripheral and semi-peripheral countries. For de Sousa Santos, the main features of economic globalization include requiring national economies to open up to trade and to privatize productive state enterprises, as well as to ensure that private property rights are clear and inviolable.[43] Simultaneous battles for the formalization of property rights and against corruption are at the core of the contemporary neo-liberal economic programme.[44]

Emerging from the wilderness years, law in development has come once again on to the international agenda, its original concern with the economic growth of the developmental state having been transmogrified into the promotion of good governance and the rule of law and, in the words of de Sousa Santos, 'formal democracy as a political condition for international assistance'.[45]

The revival of law and development has thus taken the particular form of an emphasis on the rule of law. For its advocates, the rule of law is a necessity for development.[46] Without the formalization of the legal rules governing property, for example, economic growth will be held back. In Posner's words, 'a modernizing nation's economic prosperity requires at least a modest legal infrastructure centred on the protection of property and contract rights'.[47] The World Bank's General Counsel, Ibrahim Shihata, has elaborated the elements of the rule of law as follows: a set of rules known in advance; rules that are actually in force; the existence of mechanisms to ensure the proper application of rules but which allow controlled departure when necessary; the existence of an independent judicial or arbitral body to make binding decisions when conflicts in the application of rules arise; and procedures for amending rules.[48]

Invoking de Soto, former US Secretary of State Colin Powell declared in 2002 that 'the hidden architecture of sustainable development is the law. The law. The rule of law that permits wonderful things to happen.'[49] The promotion of the rule of law is now firmly established as a priority of foreign aid. Since the 1990s, the United States and other bilateral donors as well as international financial institutions, have focused foreign aid projects increasingly on the rule of law.[50] As I show in my discussion of the World Bank in Chapter 3, 'rule of law aid' or 'rule of law reform' is now a central feature of development assistance. Such rule of law reforms are global in their reach. Although in the global context it is clear that Africa has been a minor recipient of this type of aid, land law reform has been a key area of priority for rule of law projects.

Critiques abound of the emphasis placed on the rule of law. Based on empirical and historical evidence from the United States and Japan, Upham has argued that the rule of law defies attempts to create a universal template and that it cannot be transplanted from one country to another. For Upham, the intricate connections between law and politics should not be denied but made explicit. Indeed, the imposition of the rule of law could impede economic, social and political development because the formalization of rules ignores the workings of informal agreements and social control. Upham asserts that the rule of law has been misconceived as a path to development when it should in fact be viewed as a desirable consequence of development.[51]

In a detailed critique of de Soto's programme, David Kennedy, a legal academic who has written extensively on the possible role that law might play in bringing about development, has pointed out that the many problematic aspects of de Soto's work should not be allowed to distract us from the fact that it is none the less correct 'to insist that "capital" is a legal institution'.[52] This outlook is confirmed in de Soto's insistence that: 'Property is not a primary quality of assets, but the legal expression of an

11

economically meaningful consensus about assets ... Property is not the assets themselves but a consensus between people as to how those assets should be held, used and exchanged.'[53] Exploring de Soto's ideas in the context of the recent revival in law and development, Kennedy offers an insightful characterization of the contemporary embrace of the rule of law.[54] He argues that there is an unarticulated hope among practitioners and scholars that opting for law might substitute for, and thus avoid confrontation with, 'perplexing political and economic choices'.[55] Echoing Upham's analysis, Kennedy argues that there has been a failure to interrogate 'the idea that building the rule of law might itself be a development strategy'.[56] This has meant that law and development practitioners and scholars have excluded, rather than encouraged, contestation over economic and political choices: 'this places law, legal institution building, the techniques of legal policy-making and implementation – the "rule of law" broadly conceived – front and centre'.[57]

In the next section, I draw on Kennedy's observation that reliance on the rule of law as a development strategy itself reflects economic and ideological commitments. My aim is to capture a sense both of structure and of agency in the process of land law reform and to show how we have been persuaded to overlook a range of political and economic choices by relying on the law. Land, as a social and economic asset, invites such contestation perhaps more than any other. How land may be dealt in, and by whom, is a question of social, political and economic importance. Taking our cue from Kennedy, it is necessary to explore whether in recent years contestation over the meaning and direction of land reform has been excluded by resorting to law and to building legal institutions.

Structure and agency in 'law and development'

Within the broader context of the revival of law and development, how has land law reform come to occupy a central place on the rule of law agenda? How has the project for the formalization of land relations which began in the early 1990s been articulated and promoted? Drawing on literature in the sociology of science, Bruno Latour's theory of the means by which networks are created, sustained and fall into disrepair provides us with a useful starting point.[58] By charting the success of Louis Pasteur's laboratory in isolating the anthrax virus and developing a vaccine against it, Latour showed the conditions necessary for a given discipline to establish itself initially and to thrive thereafter. Latour sought in his work to destabilize the distinction, hitherto commonly respected by social scientific accounts of science, between micro-level studies (which entailed 'studying micronegotiations inside scientific disciplines') and macro-level accounts (which involved 'studying organizations, institutions, public policy').[59] Instead, Latour argued for the need to get inside the 'sacred walls of these temples' and to recognize that 'nothing extraordinary' and nothing 'scientific' was happening.[60] The importance of Latour's contribution to the sociology of science lay in focusing 'on the construction of the lab and its position in the social milieu'.[61]

The importance of this analysis for the purpose of understanding the last two decades of land reform in Africa resides in its explicit acknowledgement and elaboration of the ways in which interests are translated and, furthermore, in its refusal to heed the boundaries between inside and outside which scientific disciplines are designed to respect. For Latour, it is precisely by respecting these boundaries that we enable mystified versions of scientific activity to be promulgated. Latour showed how Pasteur succeeded in establishing his laboratory as 'an obligatory point of passage' in a world that previously had not been exposed to laboratory science. Thus, groups with a range of different interests, such as farmers, came to see a vaccine against anthrax as the solution to their problems. Pasteur was able to enrol and enlist others by convincing them of what their interests were and what they ought to be.[62] Pasteur's microbiology was perceived to have

13

defeated the anthrax virus so the message was, 'If you wish to solve your anthrax problem, come to my lab because that's where the forces are reversed. If you don't ... you will be eliminated.'[63] Latour showed that, far from being inevitable, the central role played by Pasteur's laboratory came about because he was able to 'translate' the interests of many different actors into a scientific issue and to propagate the message that the solution to their problems lay in his laboratory.

How might we employ Latour's insights into the sociology of science to explain what has occurred in land law reform? I will argue that land law reform has become an 'obligatory point of passage'[64] for those seeking to solve Africa's development problems. Before doing so, however, it is useful to rethink the early law and development movement in this light. Drawing on network theory as elaborated by Latour enables us to understand the work of law in development scholars who crafted for themselves a central role in the post-independence developmental state. In the social sciences, such scholars sought to promote their own discipline as the discipline of the independence era.[65] In the African context, this can be explained by a particular historical conjuncture. Legal scholars moved to fill the void left by anthropology, the dominant discipline of the colonial period. Whereas anthropology had become discredited in the eyes of the leaders of newly independent states, law was relatively untainted by the colonial project. Legal solutions were thus sought to the problems of development. A prominent example of this approach was the work of Professor L. C. B. Gower in drafting a new company law in Ghana.[66] A legal training came to be considered a desirable qualification for work in the vast government bureaucracies developed after independence. In this period the implicit message was, 'If you want to solve your political, economic, institutional or intellectual problem regarding Africa, you must pass through the legal academy first.'[67]

Similarly, Latour's network theory provides us with important insights into the contemporary land law reform process.

Those who advocate legal solutions to land problems capture the interests of others, 'convincing others of what their interests are and what they ought to want and to be'.[68] In the field of land reform, as I show in Chapter 4, technical legal consultants have played a key role in advocating the resolution of land problems through the use of law. Seen in this light, the interest in land law reform which has characterized the last two decades is predominantly a consequence and not a cause of such work. Technical legal consultants have successfully intervened to assist in the difficult task of addressing contradictory demands in relation to land. The experience of Tanzania is pertinent here. In the 1980s, rural inhabitants had become increasingly vocal in pressing the government to address problems of land grabbing, as well as the chaotic state of the land tenure system. However, the main impetus for embarking on the land reform process came from international financial institutions that saw land reform as intricately connected to questions of good governance and the efficient operation of a market economy. In opting for legal solutions, the boundaries between what the international financial institutions want and what they are made to want[69] by technical legal consultants pressing for legal solutions have been increasingly blurred. As experts, the skill of land-related technical legal consultants lies in 'fostering interest groups and persuading their members that their interests were inseparable from [the consultants'] own'.[70]

Translating the interests of significant groups in the land reform process necessarily entails identifying the pertinent cause of the problem faced by African societies. This might be summed up in the following diagnosis: 'If you have lacked development, it is because you lack the rule of law which brings with it the formalization of property. Dead capital is tied up in your land that can only be liberated by formalizing tenure relations.' As I have shown above, such an analysis has widespread currency at the present time. Having designated informal land tenure as the cause of underdevelopment, the message is propagated that if the third world wants to solve its problem, it must formalize land relations by passing through what we might describe as a law laboratory.

Although an instrumentalist view of law fell out of favour in the 1970s, economic and political neo-liberalism have now provided the necessary conditions for a new law and development. Land law reform plays a central role in this new law and development. What the seemingly inexorable rise of the land reform project may obscure, however, is the difficult distributional choices which any land policy must entail. By creating and working to sustain a network of land law reform, in which priority is given to the formalization of property rights and the promotion of the rule of law, some political and economic choices will have been excluded. Drawing on Latour's work on the sociology of science, we can begin to construct an account of the last two decades of land law reform. Latour's sociology allows us to explore how law became an 'obligatory point of passage'[71] and to recover a sense of agency most often missing from accounts of land law reform.[72] In doing so, however, it is important to retain an understanding of the importance of structure. While Latour's sociology lends an important sense of agency to the last two decades, explicating how law has come to play a central role in land issues, its usefulness in accounting for the wider economic and political context within which the many important actors on the land reform scene have played out their roles is limited. One might say that whereas Latour's model assists in explaining *how* the network of African land law reform came about, it is less helpful in describing *why* this has occurred. As Byres has reminded us: '[l]and reform [does] not reach policy agendas in a political vacuum'.[73] Latour's sociology elevates the role of individuals in creating and sustaining networks and its explanatory power is limited by its emphasis on individual motivation. Although it contains an implicit suggestion that networks can only succeed at particular historical moments, political context is rarely foregrounded in Latour's network theory.

In exploring the network of African land law reform, what is required is an account of both agency and structure. Efforts to promote land law reform since the 1990s cannot be understood without attention to the wider context of contemporary economic and political neo-liberalism.

Cutler's work on the role on law in neo-liberal globalization offers a means to explore this wider context. From a historical materialist position, Cutler has argued that the significance of law's role in the process of neo-liberal globalization has not been adequately understood and critiqued.[74] Cutler notes that law links global and local political and economic orders in complex ways, forming 'a juridical link between local and global political–legal orders'[75] so that, despite being neglected in most scholarship, 'the globalisation of law is an integral aspect of the globalisation of capitalism'.[76] Law plays a crucial role in the globalization of capitalism in two interrelated ways. First, the globalization of law promotes certain values: 'the law that is globalised is essentially American or Anglo-American in origin, promoting the values of neo-liberal regulatory orders. These values and beliefs are in turn embodied in legal rules that provide the foundation for the expansion of property relations based in the private appropriation of surplus value.'[77] Second, the cultural effect of the process of globalizing law 'is integral to the internalisation of neo-liberal discipline by elites' while also ensuring that this discipline is in turn reproduced in local laws as well as transnational laws.[78] Cutler argues that 'globalised law advances the interests of a transnational class whose members function as the "organic intellectuals" for the globalisation of capitalism'[79] and that a transnational class 'advances a particular legal culture informed by neo-liberal values and the privileging of private ordering as the most natural, efficient, consensual and just means of regulating commercial and productive relations'.[80]

Although in my view Cutler's depiction of law as 'ubiquitous' – everywhere codifying and regulating economic, social and

Introduction

political life – is overdrawn, her elaboration of law's importance to the globalization of capitalism contains important insights.[81] I return to the question of law's ubiquity below, but before that I would like to elaborate on how Cutler's characterization of law might assist in understanding the functioning of a network of African land law reform. First, Cutler's theoretical approach allows us to model the different levels at which land law reform has been debated and enacted. Law forms the link between the many levels of land law reform, starting at the global level with international financial institutions and moving through national governments down to peasants in the fields. The notion of a 'juridical link' allows us to see the phenomenon of land law reform in its global and local aspects. It also enables us to recognize that the network of land law reform is not created and carefully maintained for its own sake. The globalization of law, as Cutler reminds us, is fundamental to the globalization of capitalism. Harnessing this insight to Latour's network theory allows us greater insights into the law lab and the question of why certain diagnoses are reached and certain solutions recommended. The diagnosis that the problems of economic development lie in non-formalized land relations can only take place in an era of neo-liberalism, and the solution – that land relations must be formalized – likewise has its political and economic context.

Cutler further urges us to be alert to the ways in which the globalization of law promotes certain values. The replacement of communal tenure with private tenure is achieved not simply by the spread of a network but by the globalization of law. Across Africa, remarkably similar new land laws will seek to replace complex and varied forms of communal tenure with private land tenure.[82] Whereas network theory provides a powerful account of how individuals might work to create and sustain the network which achieves this alteration in land relations, Cutler's attention to the role of elites allows us to go further to explain the endurance of networks. Local elites internalize the globalization of law, naturalizing and privileging private ordering and portraying the process of its triumph over other forms of social and economic life, such as communal tenure, as consensual. In accounting for the role of a transnational elite, the members of which act as 'organic intellectuals for the globalisation of capitalism'[83] Cutler's account allows us to explore the role of powerful actors in the land reform process.

Collateral damage

In an era of 'neo-liberal triumphalism',[84] little attention has been paid to that which is excluded by opting for one approach to African land tenure rather than another. Debates about the purpose and direction of land reform have taken place within strictly proscribed parameters. The liberalization of land is treated primarily as a technical exercise and, with the exception of a few commentators,[85] its ideological nature remains unexposed. Kennedy has prompted us to consider what is excluded when the formalization of land relations is granted lofty status as the solution to the problems of development.[86]

At least two alternative perspectives have been neglected as a result of the dominance of legal solutions to land. First, as Kennedy argues, the difficult distributional choices entailed in any debate about land have been overlooked. According to Benda-Beckmann, this amounts to treating property law as 'scapegoat and magic charm'[87] and ensures that the political aspects of property and vexed issues of redistribution are not confronted.[88] Cutler has summed up this perspective by urging us to pay attention to 'the political significance of law, in terms of determining who gets what'.[89] The second perspective that has been missing from contemporary debates about land law reform is the question of what constitutes law. De Soto and the World Bank purport to celebrate the idea that landholdings range from the purely informal to those formally recognized and given support by the legal system of the state.[90] De Soto is keen to project himself as the champion of the poor whose empirical research has recognized and recorded the struggles in which the poor engage to acquire 'accumulated assets'.[91] In his words: 'I resent the characterization of such heroic entrepreneurs as contributors to the problem of global poverty.'[92] De Soto's professed celebration of the assets of the poor should not, however, mask the fact that alternative forms of land tenure are deprecated and undervalued by advocates of formalization. Communal and informal tenure arrangements are characterized as 'passive',[93] 'defective'[94] and 'extra-legal',[95] and as belonging to 'the grubby basement of the pre-capitalist world'.[96]

The legal centralist assumptions that underpin contemporary land reform efforts have thus remained largely unexposed.[97] Legal centralism has been described as the idea that 'law is and should be the law of the state, uniform for all persons, exclusive of all other law, and administered by a single set of state institutions. To the extent that other, lesser normative orderings ... exist, they ought to be and in fact are hierarchically subordinate to the law and institutions of the state.'[98] A legal centralist outlook characterizes de Soto's work. Despite his suggestion that his approach seeks to celebrate and reward the creativity of the poor, which he describes as 'the arduous achievements of the small entrepreneur',[99] de Soto's approach to informal property rights is to categorize them as 'extralegal social contracts on property'.[100] De Soto seeks to snuff out once and for all the range of normative orders which, although they enjoy no connection to the state, play important roles in the people's lives.[101] The multitude of ways in which people relate to and perceive of land as well as their fellow landholders are denied by legal centralism. In deprecating informal land tenure arrangements as backward and economically inefficient, advocates of formalization suggest that it is only by bringing these arrangements into the formal legal system of the state that their value can be realized. This approach fails to acknowledge the multitude of ways in which people deal in land and 'fails to explain why law-like patterns of social behaviour occur even though they lack some of the apparently essential characteristics of formal law'.[102]

De Soto's programme and its World Bank counterpart also fail to acknowledge that there may be legitimate and important reasons why people choose to hold and deal in land outside the formal legal system (the 'extralegal' system to employ de Soto's term). For example, empirical research among women urban farmers who work small plots of land within the borders of many third world cities under informal arrangements has demonstrated how, even in the face of undeniable uncertainty as to their continuing access to the land, they wish to retain the advantages of informal arrangements. This allows them to evade the payment of rates and taxes and avoids the revelation of important sources of independent income to male members of their family. Faced with a physically and symbolically coercive state,[103] women and others, such as urban slum dwellers, have adopted practices of 'exit'.[104] This suggests that they have chosen 'poaching, appropriation, silence'[105] rather than visible engagement with or opposition to the state. As Davis has put it in his study of urban slums:

> The pundits of bootstrap capitalism, like the irrepressible Hernando de Soto, may see [the] enormous population of marginalized labourers, redundant civil servants and ex-peasants as actually a frenzied beehive of ambitious entrepreneurs yearning for formal property rights and unregulated competitive space, but it makes more obvious sense to consider most informal workers as the 'active' unemployed, who have no choice but to subsist by some means or starve. The world's estimated 100 million street kids are not likely – apologies to Senor de Soto – to start issuing IPOs or selling chewing-gum futures.[106]

Conclusion

I elaborate upon these themes in the remainder of this book. In Chapter 2 I explore the political and economic backdrop to

21

contemporary land reform in Africa, a process which Bernstein has dubbed 'new wave land reform in an era of neo-liberalism'.[107] I show that pressures on national governments from rural constituents to deal with long-standing problems of land conflicts have combined with the agenda of international financial institutions and bilateral donors to liberalize land tenure. It appears that once national governments began to address grievances over land, by appointing Commissions of Inquiry into land matters for example, matters began quickly to develop beyond their control.[108] There is evidence that the land reform process developed a substantial momentum of its own, ultimately leading national governments to approve new land laws over which they feel little sense of ownership or control. This explains the confusion with which new land laws are often received and the uncertainty that surrounds the questions of how they are to be implemented.

Having described the political, economic and social context of recent land reform in Chapter 2, the remaining chapters explore discrete sections of the network of land law reform. The workings of each section are explored in turn and the ways in which parts of the network interact and overlap are discussed. In Chapter 3, I discuss the role of international financial institutions in pressing for land law reform. The role of the World Bank, the key institution concerned with land issues, is explored through a study of its main policy documents. This chapter demonstrates that the World Bank has been, and will continue to be, a key actor in the network of land law reform. The World Bank has sought to address what it perceives to be the problems of land relations by using the law to bring about changes in tenure relations. Placing the World Bank's land policy in the broader context of the revival of interest in the rule of law, this chapter demonstrates that the Bank constitutes a central element of a revived network of law and development practice. It also investigates the role of bilateral aid donors in promoting land reform.

Chapter 4 goes on to discuss a further element of the revival of law and development of the network of land law reform. Technical legal consultants have played a key role in drafting new land laws that facilitate the liberalization of land tenure and have bolstered efforts to 'bring the assets of the poor into the legal system'.[109] Their role in promoting the use of the law to address land issues is explored here. In addition to drawing on Latour's sociology of science to suggest how the work of technical legal consultants on land might be modelled, this chapter explores key debates in legal methodology that have characterized the last two decades. It aims to show that contestation about the role of law and about the methodology to be adopted in drafting new land laws, far from being technical debates among lawyers, are intricately connected with political choices.

In Chapter 5, the ambiguous role of civil society groups during the last decade of land reform is discussed. Such groups have been an important element of the network of land law reform. Drawing in particular on the experiences of gender progressive groups in Tanzania and Uganda during the land reform process, I show that rather than challenging the use of law and the exclusion of distributional choices that this has entailed, civil society groups have themselves adopted a technicist and instrumentalist approach to land issues. Rather than debating and challenging the direction of land reform, they have been largely reactive, commenting on new legislation and pressing for amendments to the law. They have not shown themselves effective in influencing the broader policy agenda. In Chapter 5, I suggest reasons to explain this and contrast their impact and strategies with those of emerging rural movements in Africa.

In Chapter 6, I explore the lessons that can be drawn from the last two decades of land reform in Africa and discuss some of the implications of the changes in land tenure we have witnessed. Having traced in the course of this book the privatization of land and the process of its marketization, as well as the vigorous efforts directed at financializing land relations, I discuss in this chapter what I see as the emerging struggles of the future. I identify three likely future developments. First, I suggest that the coming years will witness a worsening of gender relations as, increasing land-related debt puts pressure on women's unpaid household labour. Second, I point out that the prominent roles that will come to be played by commercial lenders and the judiciary have received no attention to date. Yet it is clear that bankers' organizations have already had an important impact on determining the shape and content of Africa's new land laws. The liberalization of land markets and the promotion of formal credit provide unprecedented opportunities for commercial lenders in Africa. Their lobbying activities have had a powerful impact on the process of land tenure reform as they have tried to ensure that new land laws do not increase the risks entailed in lending. I suggest that they will continue to exert even greater influence in the future and that the promotion of rural credit will receive concerted backing from international donors and African governments. It can be predicted that, over the coming years, the judiciary will play an increasingly important role in African land matters as it seeks ways to fulfil the demands of commercial lenders for certainty in lending. Chapter 6 also seeks to demonstrate, third, that although it has been largely neglected in discussions of land law reform, the issue of implementation merits close study. The dominant approach to implementation has been to see it as the relatively unproblematic end-point of the process of reform. This technical approach has overlooked the important role of implementers of land law, 'the street level bureaucrats',[110] whose attitude to new laws can have a dramatic impact on their prospects. I argue that the difficulties of implementation – which, having been neglected in the course of debates about new land laws, have recently begun to receive the attention of policy-makers – will become an increasingly important feature of the African land question in coming years.

Notes

1 Former US President Bill Clinton's Address to the British Labour Party Conference, October 2002. Full text available at <politics.guardian.co.uk/labour2002> (accessed December 2005).

2 A. Callinicos, *An Anti-Capitalist Manifesto* (Cambridge: Polity, 2003).

3 A. Callinicos, *Against the Third Way* (Cambridge: Polity, 2001), p. 2.

4 See Institute for Liberty and Democracy at <www.ild.org.pe/home.htm> (accessed December 2005).

5 H. de Soto, *The Mystery of Capital: Why Capitalism Triumphs in the West and Fails Everywhere Else* (London: Black Swan, 2000).

6 Ibid., p. 32.

7 Ibid., p. 6.

8 Ibid.

9 Ibid., p. 7.

10 Ibid.

11 Ibid., p. 12.

12 Ibid., p. 9.

13 See <www.imf.org/external/pubs/tt/fandd/2003/12/pdf/people.pdf> (accessed December 2005).

14 de Soto, *The Mystery of Capital*, p. 164.

15 Ibid., p. 46.

16 Ibid., p. 60.

17 World Bank, *Policy Research Report: Land Policies for Growth and Poverty Reduction* (Oxford: Oxford University Press, 2003).

18 Julian Quan, Land Policy Adviser, DfID, personal communication, December 2003. See also 'Fine Words, Flawed Idea', *Guardian*, 11 September 2000; available at <www.guardian.co.uk/Archive/Article/0,4273,4061838,00.html> (accessed December 2005).

19 'Ghana: Foundation for Building the Capital of the Poor', *Accra Daily Mail*, 20 September 2002; available at <www.africaonline.com/site/Articles/1,3,4,49613.jsp> (accessed December 2005).

20 See 'Ghana to Solve Mystery of Capital'; available at <www.afrol.com/News2002/gha021_property_register.htm> (accessed December 2005). Also, 'Bill Clinton Helps Ghana's Poor Gain Property Titles'; available at <www.undp.org/dpa/frontpagearchive/2002/october/7oct> (accessed December 2005).

21 Quoted in ibid.

22 World Bank, *Land Reform: Sector Policy Paper* (Washington, DC: World Bank, 1975); N. Stern, 'Foreword', in World Bank, *Land Policies for Growth*, pp. ix–xi. See also K. Deininger and H. Binswanger, 'The Evolution of the World Bank's Land Policy: Principles, Experiences

25

and Future Challenges', *World Bank Research Observer*, 14 (1999), pp. 247–76.

23 World Bank, 'Electronic Conference on Land Policy and Sustainable Development', 2001. For details, see <www.oxfam.org.uk/landrights/Donormtg.rtf> (accessed December 2005).

24 World Bank, *Land Policies for Growth*.

25 R. Palmer, 'A Guide to and Some Comments on, the World Bank's Policy Research Report: Land Policy for Pro-Poor Growth and Development'; <Inweb18.worldbank.org.ESSD/essdext.nsf/24ByDocName/PRRe-Discussion> (accessed December 2005).

26 Organizations that signed the open letter included the National Land Committee; Rural Development Services Network; Landless People's Movement; Transkei Land Service Organization; Southern Africa Network on Land; and Trust for Community Outreach and Education. See 'Open Letter to the World Bank on the Land Policy "Consultation": An African Appeal'; available at <www.nlc.co.za/pubs/wbopenletter02.htm> (accessed December 2005).

27 World Bank, *Land Policies for Growth*, pp. xix–xx.

28 Ibid., p. 40.

29 Ibid., pp. 48–51.

30 Ibid., pp. xix and xx.

31 Ibid., xxxvi–xxxvii.

32 *The Economist*, 'Breathing Life into Dead Capital: Why Secure Property Rights Matter', in *How to Make Africa Smile: A Survey of Sub-Saharan Africa*, 17 January 2004, pp. 10–11.

33 World Bank, *Land Policies for Growth*.

34 Callinicos, *An Anti-Capitalist Manifesto*, p. 3.

35 For a discussion of this approach in the context of land tenure, see I. Yngstrom, 'Women, Wives and Land Rights in Africa: Situating Gender Beyond the Household in the Debate Over Land Policy and Changing Tenure Systems', *Oxford Development Studies*, 30 (1) (2002), pp. 21–40.

36 World Bank, *Land Policies for Growth*, pp. 62–5.

37 Y. Ghai, 'Law, Development and African Scholarship', *Modern Law Review*, 50 (1987), pp. 750–76. See also Y. Vyas, K. Kibwana, O. Owiti and S. Wanjala, *Law and Development in the Third World* (Nairobi: Faculty of Law, 1994).

38 D. Trubek and M. Galanter, 'Scholars in Self-Estrangement: Some Reflections on the Crisis in Law and Development Studies in the United States', *Wisconsin Law Review* (1974), pp. 1062–101.

39 S. Amin, *Capitalism in the Age of Globalization: The Management of Contemporary Society* (London: Zed Books, 2000), p. 32.

40 J. Merryman, 'Comparative Law and Social Change: On the

Origins, Style, Decline and Revival of the Law and Development Movement', *American Journal of Comparative Law*, 25 (1977), pp. 457–83.

41 U. Baxi, 'Global Development and Impoverishment', in P. Cane and M. Tushnet (eds), *Oxford Handbook of Legal Studies* (Oxford: Oxford University Press, 2003), pp. 455–82; T. Ginsburg, 'Does Law Matter for Economic Development: Evidence from East Asia', *Law and Society Review*, 34 (3) (2000), pp. 829–56; M. Chibundu, 'Law in Development: On Tapping, Gourding and Serving Palm-Wine', *Case Western Reserve Journal of International Law*, 29 (1) (1997), pp. 167–258.

42 B. Spalling, *Development with Equity in the 1990s: Policies and Alternatives* (Madison, WI: Global Studies Research Programme, 1992).

43 B. de Sousa Santos, *Toward a New Legal Common Sense: Law, Globalization, and Emancipation* (London: Butterworths, 2002).

44 D. Kennedy, 'Laws and Developments', in A. Perry and J. Hatchard (eds), *Law and Development: Facing Complexity in the 21st Century* (London: Cavendish, 2003). See also A. Manji, '"The Beautyful Ones" of Law and Development', in D. Buss and A. Manji (eds), *International Law: Modern Feminist Approaches* (Oxford: Hart Publishing, 2005), pp. 159–71.

45 de Sousa Santos, *Toward a New Legal Common Sense*, p. 167.

46 J. Sachs, 'Globalisation and Employment', Public lecture to International Labor Organization, 1996; available at <ilo.org/public/english/bureau/inst/papers/publecs/sachs/ch2.htm> (accessed December 2005).

47 R. Posner, 'Creating a Legal Framework for Economic Development', *World Bank Research Observer*, 13 (1) (1998), pp. 1–11.

48 I. Shihata, *Complementary Reforms: Essays on Legal, Judicial and Other Institutional Reforms Supported by the World Bank* (Boston, MA: Kluwer Law International, 1997).

49 See Institute for Liberty and Democracy at <www.ild.org.pe/home.htm> (accessed December 2005).

50 J. Perelman, 'The Way Ahead: Access to Justice, Public Interest Lawyering and the Right to Legal Aid in South Africa: The Nkuzi Case', *Stanford Journal of International Law*, 41 (1) (forthcoming).

51 F. Upham, 'Ideology, Experience and the Rule of Law in Developing Societies', Paper presented at a round table on the Rule of Law at the Carnegie Endowment, 5 September 2001.

52 Kennedy, 'Laws and Developments', pp. 17–35. See also A. C. Cutler, 'Historical Materialism, Globalization, and Law: Competing Conceptions of Property', in M. Rupert and H. Smith (eds), *Historical Materialism and Globalization* (London: Routledge, 2002), pp. 230–56, 233.

53 de Soto, *The Mystery of Capital*, p. 164.

54 Kennedy, 'Laws and Developments'.

55 Ibid., p. 17.

56 Ibid. (author's emphasis).

57 Ibid., p. 18.

58 B. Latour, 'Give Me a Laboratory and I Will Raise the World', in K. D. Knorr-Cetina and M. Mulkay (eds), *Science Observed: Perspectives in the Social Study of Science* (London: Sage, 1983).

59 Ibid., p. 142.

60 Ibid., p. 141.

61 Ibid., p. 142.

62 Ibid., p. 143.

63 Ibid., p. 147.

64 Ibid., p. 146.

65 J. Harrington and A. Manji, 'The Emergence of African Law as an Academic Discipline in Britain', *African Affairs*, 102 (2003), pp. 109–34.

66 L. C. B. Gower, *Final Report of the Commission of Enquiry into the Working and Administration of the Present Company Law of Ghana* (Accra: Government of Ghana, 1961). I discuss Gower's work in greater detail in Chapter 4.

67 Harrington and Manji, 'The Emergence of African Law', pp. 109–34.

68 Latour, 'Give Me a Laboratory', p. 144.

69 Ibid.

70 Ibid., p. 150.

71 Ibid.

72 A. Manji, 'Cause and Consequence in Law and Development', *Journal of Modern African Studies*, 43 (1) (2005), pp. 119–38.

73 T. J. Byres, 'Introduction: Contextualizing and Interrogating the GKI Case for Redistributive Land Reform', *Journal of Agrarian Change*, 4 (1–2) (2004), pp. 1–16, 3.

74 Cutler, 'Historical Materialism', pp. 230–56.

75 Ibid., p. 231.

76 Ibid.

77 Ibid.

78 Ibid.

79 Ibid.

80 Ibid.

81 For a differing account of law's ubiquity, see A. Manji, 'Imagining Women's "Legal World": Towards a Feminist Theory of Legal Pluralism in Africa', *Social and Legal Studies*, 8 (4) (1999) pp. 435–55.

82 B. Cousins and A. Claassens, 'Communal Tenure "From Above" and "From Below": Land Rights, Authority and Livelihoods in Rural South Africa', in S. Evers, M. Spierenburg and H. Wels (eds), *Competing Jurisdictions: Settling Land Claims in Africa* (Leiden: Brill, 2005).

83 Cutler, 'Historical Materialism', p. 231.

84 H. Bernstein, 'Land Reform: Taking a Long(er) View', *Journal of Agrarian Change*, 1 (2002), pp. 433–63.

85 I. G. Shivji, 'Guest Editor's Introduction: Not Yet Uhuru', *Change*, 5 (1997), pp. 2–3; G. Sundet, *The Politics of Land in Tanzania*, Unpublished D. Phil. Thesis, University of Oxford, 1997.

86 Kennedy, 'Laws and Developments'.

87 F. von Benda-Beckmann, 'Scapegoat and Magic Charm: Law in Development Theory and Practice', *Journal of Legal Pluralism and Unofficial Law and Unofficial Law*, 28 (1989), pp. 129–48.

88 F. von Benda-Beckmann, 'Mysteries of Capital or Mystification of Legal Property?', *Focaal: European Journal of Anthropology*, 41 (2003), pp. 187–91.

89 Cutler, 'Historical Materialism', p. 231.

90 F. von Benda Beckman, 'Legal Pluralism and Social Justice in Economic and Political Development', Paper presented at a Workshop on the Rule of Law and Development, Institute of Development Studies, 1–3 June 2000; P. Houtzager, '"We Make the Law and the Law Makes Us": Some Ideas on a Law in Development Research Agenda', *IDS Bulletin*, 32 (1) (2001), pp. 8–18.

91 de Soto, *The Mystery of Capital*, p. 12.

92 Ibid., p. 34.

93 Ibid., p. 6.

94 Ibid.

95 Ibid., p. 191.

96 Ibid., p. 55.

97 But see von Benda Beckman, 'Legal Pluralism and Social Justice'.

98 J. Griffiths, 'What is Legal Pluralism?', *Journal of Legal Pluralism and Unofficial Law*, 24 (1986), pp. 1–55.

99 Ibid., p. 164.

100 Ibid., p. 181.

101 M. Galanter, 'Justice in Many Rooms: Courts, Private Ordering, and Indigenous Law', *Journal of Legal Pluralism and Unofficial Law*, 19 (1981), pp. 30–42.

102 H. W. Arthurs, *Without the Law: Administrative Justice and Legal Pluralism in Nineteenth Century England* (Toronto: University of Toronto Press, 1985), p. ix.

103 See Manji, 'Imagining Women's "Legal World"', pp. 435–55.

104 R. Fatton, 'Gender, Class and State in Africa', in J. Parpart and K. Staudt (eds) *Women and the State in Africa* (London: Lynne Rienner, 1989), pp. 47–66.

105 P. Ewick and S. Silbey, 'Conformity, Contestation and Resist-

ance: An Account of Legal Consciousness', *New England Law Review*, 26 (1992), pp. 73–89.

106 M. Davis, 'Planet of the Slums: Urban Involution and the Informal Proletariat', *New Left Review*, 26 (2004), pp. 5–36. See also T. Mitchell, 'The Properties of Markets: Informal Housing and Capitalism's Mystery', *Cultural Political Economy Working Paper* No. 2 (University of Lancaster: Institute for Advanced Studies in Social and Management Sciences, n.d.).

107 H. Bernstein, 'Land Reform: Taking a Long(er) View', *Journal of Agrarian Change* (2002), pp. 433–63.

108 L. Wily, 'Changing Property Relations of State and People: A Critical Review of Land Reform in Eastern and Southern Africa at the Turn of the Century', Unpublished paper on file with the author.

109 Former US President Bill Clinton's Address to the British Labour Party Conference, October 2002.

110 R. A. Weatherley, *Reforming Special Education: Policy Implementation from State Level to Street Level* (Boston, MA: MIT Press, 1979).

2 Contemporary land reform in Africa

There is a palpable sense of surprise and bemusement in the air when the prospects for Africa's new land laws are being discussed. The impression given is that new laws are being imposed with unseemly haste, causing confusion among those affected by them. Puzzled questions are being asked: how did we end up with these new laws? How are we to deal with the changes they bring?

The emergence of land reform on to national political agendas in the late 1980s can be understood only in the context of wider pressures for the liberalization of African economies.[1] While African states were no doubt under pressure from rural constituents to deal with grievances over land matters, to address historical wrongs or to resolve problems of conflict and displacement, this does not fully account for the thorough overhaul in land relations that resulted a few years later. Before elaborating on the rise to prominence of land law reform, in this chapter I explore some of the problems concerning land being experienced on the continent and discuss the issue of what Africa's land questions might be. I begin by investigating the broader issue of why land reform is perceived to be important and by addressing the question: what precisely do we mean by land reform?

Defining land reform

Land reform has a long history[2] and both socialist and non-socialist states have attached importance to land relations as a marker of broader economic and political relations. Byres, arguing that land tenure was often perceived as an impediment to growth in the post-1945 period, cites an early United Nations report on land reform as evidence: 'for many countries the agrarian structure, and in particular systems of land tenure, prevent a rise in the standard of living of small farmers and agricultural labourers and impede economic development, both by preventing the expansion of the food supply and by causing agriculture – usually the major economic activity – to stagnate.'[3] According to this view, the economy as a whole, not just the agrarian sector, is adversely affected by inequitable or inefficient tenure. From what has been described as an inter-sectoral perspective,[4] it is argued that problems in agriculture affect the growth not just of this sector of the economy but of industry as well. Unsatisfactory land tenure is held responsible for a lack of economic growth by restricting food supplies to the urban workforce, as well as by allowing the countryside to stagnate.

More recently, discourses of international development aid have explicitly linked access to secure property rights with poverty reduction. As I show in Chapter 3, the World Bank has been at the forefront of propagating the idea that unclear tenure rights hinder the development of agricultural and wider credit markets and it has been joined in this view by bilateral donors, with the UK, acting through the Department for International Development (DfID), chief among them. In addition, as I will show, the report of Britain's Commission for a Strong and Prosperous Africa has urged that all donors support the acquisition of formal legal title to land in order to tackle poverty and promote growth.[5] Land issues are now clearly visible on international aid agendas and, what is more, they take a discernible form: the encouragement of private, individual and registered property rights.

Different meanings have been attached to the term 'land reform' at different times and it is important to clarify what is meant by its use in varied contexts. In providing a historical overview of land reform, Bernstein has traced the transition from the state-led development perspectives of the 1950s and 1960s to contemporary land reform, which he describes as 'self-styled "new wave" agrarian reform in the age of neo-liberalism'.[6] Bernstein shows how the end of the developmental era also marked the cessation of major redistributive land reforms. These lasted from 1910 to 1970. For Bernstein, these reforms were part of the transition from feudalism to capitalism. A transition occurs from an agrarian to an industrial economy in which generalized commodity production is the norm. In the classic bourgeois view, agrarian change is overseen by the state in order to ensure the modernization of farming and overall economic growth. In contrast, contemporary land reform takes place in an era of globalization in which the state is taken to play a diminished role, and the liberalization of trade has integrated third world farmers into global commodity chains and markets.[7] Today, land reform is centred on property rights and has as its central aim the achievement of tenure reform, as the following account of Latin America shows:

> One of the pillars of neo-liberal thinking about the future of
> the agricultural sector is the need to provide security of tenure
> to producers to encourage investment and, hence, productivity
> and production increases. This is one of the main motivations
> behind land-titling projects and efforts to modernize cadastral
> systems and land registries. The other motivation is to foster
> a more efficient land market, making it easier for land to be
> purchased and sold. Almost every single Latin American country
> was undertaking land-titling programmes of some sort in the
> 1990s ... Once properties are measured and mapped and titles
> registered, land ownership will be more difficult to contest.[8]

It is interesting to note briefly that the timeframe set out by Bernstein in explaining these two phases of agrarian reform map on to the history of the law and development movement I have narrated in Chapter 1. It is significant that law and development's first blooming took place in the developmental era – that is, in the immediate post-independence era when redistributive reform was, in Bernstein's view, very much on the political agenda – but

33

that as an area of scholarship as well as a significant practical field, law and development ceased to have a notable impact in the 1970s. Today, both land reform and law and development have returned to the political agenda. They have both taken new forms and have reappeared in a significantly altered economic and political context. In its new guise, land reform no longer signifies *redistributive reform* with its emphasis on the possibilities of transferring larger operational holdings to those with little or no land, such as wage labourers or the landless. Instead, land reform has come to mean *tenurial reform*. Such reform is concerned with the terms on which an operational holding is controlled and worked.[9] I discuss this distinction in greater detail below but it is interesting to note here that just as the new law and development no longer takes developmentalism as its focus but has, in its new guise, instead embraced the achievement of the rule of law and good governance as the solution to the perceived problems of the third world, so in relation to land reform the current focus is not on redistributive reform but on altering land tenure. Specifically, as Sam Moyo has pointed out, discussions of land reform have focused on the problems of land administration systems and the need for their reform rather than on redistribution.[10] Finally, it is important to acknowledge that both land reform and law and development have made their reappearances in economic circumstances quite different to those that prevailed in the 1960s and 1970s. Most notably, economic globalization has forced countries of the south to open up their national economies to trade, as well as to privatize productive state enterprises.[11] As a result, 'hegemonic states, by themselves or through the international institutions they control – particularly the international financial institutions – have strained the political autonomy and the effective sovereignty of peripheral and semi-peripheral states to an unprecedented extent'.[12]

The first law and development movement had a remote relationship with redistributive land reform.[13] Both shared an overall concern with state-led development but law and development did not play a key role in the alteration of land relations in the immediate post-independence period. It is clear that today a revived law and development agenda enjoys a more intimate relationship with land reform: scholars located in the broad field of law and development debate the purpose and direction of land reform as well as frequently being involved in the technical task of drafting new land laws. In order to explain law and development's engagement in this field, it is necessary to return to the definitions of land reform introduced above and to ask: what is meant by land reform in different contexts and how is the term employed today?

In any discussion of land reform, it is important to distinguish between redistributive land reform and tenurial land reform. Byres has sought to contrast the different elements of each approach.[14] Redistributive reform is concerned with the possibilities of redistributing operational holdings, transferring land from those with larger holdings to the landless or to wage labourers for example. It thus has the potential to be more radical than tenurial reform which is concerned with the terms on which an operational holding is controlled and worked, and is attentive to those aspects of tenure which are thought to affect incentives, investment and efficiency. Both redistributive reform and tenurial reform focus on obstacles to agricultural productivity. The former holds that access to land will bring about increases in output and provide a source of subsistence and access to credit, while the latter emphasizes how certain aspects of tenure, such as tenancy arrangements, can act as impediments to growth. Calls for redistributive reform also tend to follow a period of political upheaval, for example on the achievement of national independence or as a result of peasants' demands. According to Byres, the beneficiaries of tenurial reform tend to be larger peasants, while those of any redistributive measures are generally the landless and waged labourers.

Although the potential role that law might play in these two types of land reform is not an explicit concern for Byres in his elaboration of the elements of tenurial and redistributive reform, the implications for law are evident. Redistributive reforms require that tenure reform be undertaken after the allocation of land, to consolidate or guarantee the changes. Whereas its initial impetus is political rather than legal, redistributive reform implies law reform because legal changes will be necessary in order to consolidate its achievement. In contrast, tenurial reform may also have political motivations (such as addressing the grievances of rural constituents) but it will be much more closely linked to legal change. Tenure reform is in fact land law reform. It does not require redistribution of land holdings but is dependent on the alteration of the terms on which such holdings are owned, controlled and dealt in. This will not only require changes *in* the law but will in fact be achieved *through* law.

The relative desirability of redistributive reform and tenurial reform has been much discussed by theorists of agrarian relations over the past twenty-five years. The debate has recently been reignited as the idea of poverty alleviation has come to prominence in discourses of international development.[15] The possibility of such a connection is suggested, for example, by the title of a recent paper by Keith Griffin, Azizur Rahman Khan and Amy Ickowitz that explicitly links issues of poverty and land distribution.[16] The paper prompted a vigorous debate in the pages of the *Journal of Agrarian Change*, in which Byres – from the historical materialist perspective that characterizes what is labelled the SOAS school of agrarian studies[17] – sets out what appeared to him to be the conceptual and political shortcomings of the GKI (that is, Griffin, Khan and Ickowitz) thesis on redistribution.

In essence, GKI assert that the solution to enduring rural poverty is redistributive land reform that transfers land from landlords to small peasants and landless labourers. This, according to the GKI thesis, will set up an agrarian structure dominated by peasant owner-cultivators using family labour to cultivate the land. The authors argue that tenure reform alone cannot tackle poverty or substitute for redistribution because it is possible for powerful landowners simply to ignore or find ways around tenurial changes such as the imposition of land ceilings. The GKI thesis in favour of redistribution is founded on the idea of the inverse relationship. This holds that whereas large landholders have plentiful access to land and capital, they find themselves short of sufficient labour, whereas the opposite is the case for small farmers for whom land and capital are in short supply but labour is abundant. I will discuss the gender implications of this model in Chapter 6 – emphasizing the fact that theorists of the inverse relationship can assume an abundant labour supply for small farms because they rely on the existence of unpaid family labour, and especially the efforts of women – but first it is important to explore the GKI thesis further. According to this model, large landowners respond to shortfalls in labour supply by employing expensive hired labour and by relying on mechanization to cultivate their land in an extensive manner. In contrast, small farmers cultivate their land intensively, and generate more 'employment' per unit of land. In the absence of economies of scale, this means that small landholders achieve more per unit than large ones. It is based on this perceived efficiency of small farms that GKI frame their argument for redistribution. They contend that land should be redistributed to small farmers who make more efficient use of labour and who, given greater access to capital, are likely to be more productive overall than large landholders. GKI's position is summed up in the statement that 'the case for land reform rests not on the existence of defective tenure contracts but on the concentration of land ownership rights and the inefficiency, inequality and poverty that this creates'.[18]

Byres disagrees with the GKI position on a number of grounds.[19] First, the scheme advocated by GKI would require substantial intervention by the state, an idea which Byres points out is not likely to find favour with neo-classical economists, despite GKI's liberal use of neo-classical economic concepts such as utility maximization and perfect competition. Byres charges GKI with developing a populist, utopian and ahistorical approach that ignores the importance of the industrial sector of the economy in reducing poverty. He also writes of their approach that it neglects the possible existence of capitalist relationships in the countryside and the potential that the peasant family farms envisaged in the GKI scheme may over time be transformed into capitalist farms. Byres's critique of the inverse relationship is that it misunderstands the supposed economic superiority of small farms, which might be caused not by their natural efficiency but because economic distress requires them to increase and intensify their labour input. For Byres, tenure reform alone has the potential to achieve a great deal – by abolishing landlordism, for example – and should not be wholly dismissed as it is in the GKI thesis.

The salience of the redistribution versus tenurial reform debate does not lie solely in the fact that international development discourse has recently espoused ideas of poverty reduction that also appear to be a concern of theorists of land reform. The emergence of rural movements struggling to access land through extra-legal means such as occupation or squatting also lends urgency to the discussion. As a result of land occupations, calls for redistribution have in recent years come to political prominence not just in Africa but globally. They have signalled the political and economic importance of land reform and their import has not been lost on international donors and financial institutions. The strategies adopted by Brazil's Movimiento Rural Sem Terra (Landless Workers' Movement) in the south and south-east of the country since the 1980s – including the invasion of land and its settlement, the setting up of cooperatives to oversee production, and the nurturing of alliances with the Workers' Party – is thought to have elicited a response from the World Bank and the United States Agency for International Development (USAID) in the form of accelerated titling programmes to counter the confiscatory methods of the movement.[20] I return to a discussion of rural social movements in Chapter 5 and in particular to their potential for contesting the emphasis on law that characterizes contemporary land reform.

African land questions

In this section, I explore some of the land problems experienced in African countries, such as concentration of ownership, lack of access and land disputes. In exploring the question of why land reform came on to national political agendas at this time, it is important to be alert to the range of land problems facing rural constituents and the nature of their grievances. Although, as I will show in later chapters, it has been more powerful actors such as international financial institutions that have succeeded in determining the direction of African land reform, it is important to remind ourselves of the neglected demands of rural inhabitants and of their concerns over land. These demands are evidence that there are difficult land questions facing the continent, contrary to the view of some scholars that this is an issue of little relevance outside the former settler colonies with their unique experience of land expropriation.[21] It has been argued that whereas agrarian questions surely exist on the continent (characterized as it is by food insecurity, exploitation of labour and unequal terms of trade),[22] no land question can be identified because in sub-Saharan Africa land is abundantly available and rights to such land are guaranteed by rules of customary tenure.[23]

As Moyo has pointed out, this assumption has rarely been challenged and as a result, 'the essence of [the] land question … has never been adequately conceptualised'.[24] Moyo therefore asks directly 'whether Africa has a land question, and if so, what is the nature of its land question'.[25] He argues that theorists have focused too narrowly on the root of possible land questions, seeking evidence of historical land alienation under colonialism as their first point of reference. In doing so, they have neglected the range of ways in which land concentration has taken place over time and failed to recognize the glaring empirical evidence that land inequalities due to such concentration continue to increase. Moyo points in particular to emerging rural movements as evidence of the existence of pressing African land questions.[26]

A number of scholars have sought to capture the range and complexity of Africa's land problems. In general, they have pointed to insecurity of tenure, subdivision of land, informal land markets, the alienation of land and its concentration, and the role of undemocratic structures of local government in dealing with land disputes.[27] In a recent overview, Peters provided a detailed summary of the situation:

> Competition over land for different purposes intensifies due to growing populations and movements of people looking for better/more land or fleeing civil disturbances; rural groups seek to intensify commodity production and food production while retrenched members of a downsized salariat look for land to improve food and income options; states demarcate forestry and other reserves, and identify areas worthy of conservation ... representatives of the state and political elites appropriate land through means ranging from the questionable to the illegal; and valuable resources both on and under the land (timber, oil, gold, other minerals) attract intensifying exploitation by agents from the most local (unemployed youth or erstwhile farmers seeking ways to obtain cash) to transnational networks (of multinational corporations, foreign governments and representatives of African states).[28]

In relation to common lands, Camilla Toulmin has described a 'new tragedy of the commons' in which:

> Across the continent, a land grab is under way. Governments take small farmers' land to create enterprise zones. Customary chiefs reap fortunes from urban sprawl by getting rid of 'tenants'

to make way for residential development. In Côte d'Ivoire local people seize land back from migrant farmers, who thought they had bought it. And the commons – whether grazing, woodlands, or wetlands – are being eaten away by enclosure, depriving the poorest people of their final resort when times are tough.[29]

The dependence of the poor on the commons increased in the wake of structural adjustment programmes that saw both farm and non-farm sources of income decline. Now threatened by the processes of land alienation described by Toulmin, the lack of access by the poor to natural resources constitutes a pressing contemporary land problem.

Focusing specifically on the politics of emerging rural movements and on processes of illegal land occupation or squatting, Sam Moyo presents the following analysis:

> The dominance of external financial and development aid institutions in Africa's policy making processes and markets is organic to most of the emergent land conflicts. Pressures for the growing marketisation of land reflect both external interests in economic liberalisation and foreign access to land and natural resources, as well as the increasing internal class struggles over primitive accumulation by a broadening African indigenous capitalist class. New land policies justify these tendencies of unequal land control, but generate growing conflicts over land allocation and use across class, gender, nationality and ethnic line.[30]

For Moyo, the existence of an African land question cannot be doubted. For him, 'variegated struggles at varying scales and localities over escalating unequal access to and control of land represent a real land question in ... Africa'.[31]

Broadly speaking, African land questions can be distinguished by region. Whereas North Africa has experienced severe shortages of arable land, in West Africa the problem is predominantly one of land administration and conflict between the state and local communities. In former settler colonies, the land questions arising can be seen to be connected with the concentration of resources and therefore with the issue of redistribution. Although it is thus possible to describe African land problems by employing a series of generalized and distinct explanatory categories – such as conflict arising from historical injustices or from concentration and commercialization – land issues have rarely lent themselves to such tidy portrayals. Instead, considerable overlaps can be found in the experiences of any one region or country. In Kenya, for example, the land claims being asserted by the Maasai might be categorized as arising from historical injustices, as much as from the concentration and commercialization of land for the purposes of tourism. Encapsulated in the story of the Maasai land claim is the desire to resolve historical grievances (the alienation of ancestral land by members of the community in the form of long leases to the British colonial power)[32] and ongoing dispossession due to commercialization (the long-standing development of ranching and luxury tourist facilities in Maasailand).[33] In the country as a whole, the main concern being expressed relates to the chaotic state of land administration and management, a fact that was acknowledged by the report of the Commission of Inquiry into the Land Law System (known widely as the Njonjo Commission) and the recommendations of the Constitution of Kenya Review Commission.[34]

Whatever the experiences giving rise to distinctive land questions in any given part of the continent, it is clear that, by the end of the 1980s, there had developed in many countries severe dissatisfaction over the state of land relations. It was widely felt that when opportunities to voice grievances arose, they often went unheard or in some instances prompted ad hoc and largely ineffectual government responses, often aggravating conditions such as uncertainty over tenure. As multiparty elections began to take place, it became clear that the hitherto piecemeal approach to resolving land problems had failed. McAuslan has suggested that the transition to multiparty democracy was to some extent connected with the desire of governments to be seen to be responding to concerns over land: 'the pressure to act is, at least in part, the result of contested democratic politics and the perceived need to meet the concerns of rural voters'.[35] According to Wily, it became apparent at this stage in many countries that the lack of a coherent response to land issues was no longer tolerable and that an overall review of land tenure should therefore be attempted. Explaining this situation and the momentum to which it gave rise, Wily has argued convincingly that the

> [r]easons for launching land reform tend to accumulate over time and build into a commitment to overhaul the whole rather than to amend in piecemeal ways. Immediate motivations vary widely, from frustration with shortfalls in the colonial-derived property laws, a desire to free up the market in land, accelerate entitlement programmes, or to redress land losses caused by racially discriminatory law.[36]

Chronologies of land reform

Any attempt to provide a neat temporal categorization of Africa's new land laws is bound to be defeated. Land reform has been undertaken by numerous African countries, one country after another succumbing to the process of review of land laws and the enactment of new legislation since the early 1990s. Nevertheless, within the candidate countries, land reform has not taken place in a uniformly linear fashion. Instead, the pace of change has been uneven, the process often fractured and incoherent. A telling example is Malawi's experience of finding itself faced with a new land law prior to having conducted a national debate on and approved a national land policy.[37] In this way it reversed what might be viewed as the more traditional approach of Tanzania where events took place in a more straightforward sequence: the steps involved appointing a commission of inquiry into land matters, drafting and approving a national land policy, producing a draft bill and ultimately passing new laws in the form of the Land Act 1998 and Village Land Act 1998.[38] More often, however, the land reform process has resembled a mountain route: switchbacks on a steep, barely visible path.

It is notable that in Tanzania the voices of the intended beneficiaries of land reform were indeed heard for a brief period as a result of the work of the Presidential Commission of Inquiry into Land Matters. The Commission subsequently ensured that these stories would be available to posterity by archiving and depositing their detailed findings in the University of Dar es Salaam library.[39] This attempt to capture the subaltern voices of poor subsistence farmers and rural inhabitants was itself an important contribution in a contemporary land reform process more commonly characterized by the fond use of inaccessible internet consultations and by geographically and intellectually remote technicist approaches to land. The needs articulated by Tanzania's villagers were to be lost in a process of land reform that, far from delivering the security of tenure and access to productive land desired by the poor, has led to greater insecurity and risk.

The Tanzanian story of land reform, which began in the 1990s, may be taken in many respects to be an exemplar of the contemporary African land reform process. After many years of unsatisfactory tinkering with land tenure that in most instances succeeded only in worsening tenure security, the Tanzanian government decided to undertake a thorough overhaul of the country's land laws. In doing so, the government was responding to pressure from rural constituents although the full extent and nature of their grievances would not become apparent until later. In January 1991, the government appointed a Presidential Commission of Inquiry into Land Matters. The Commission, which had as its chair Professor Issa Shivji, a law professor at the University of Dar es Salaam, travelled widely within the country and made research visits to Zimbabwe, Kenya and Eritrea in order to investigate the systems of land tenure at work in these countries.[40]

The Report of the Shivji Commission made a number of key recommendations that had the explicit goal of increasing security of tenure for the peasant producer. These were, inter alia, that radical title to land be divested from the government and vested in the village assemblies and an extra-executive body to be called the National Commission of Lands, and also that the powerful Ministry of Lands be abolished.[41] The objective of the Commission's report was not the operationalization of a land market; instead, it sought accurately to reflect the many land problems about which it had heard evidence and to answer the grievances of land users 'from below'.[42] It sought to respond to what it heard in its extensive consultation with villagers around the country by controlling the alienation of land and putting in place mechanisms to guarantee security of tenure for peasant producers.

The government did not look with pleasure on recommendations that would abolish its monopoly of the radical title to land and thereby substantially alter the structure of the state. It reacted by refraining from issuing a White Paper setting out its response to the Commission's recommendations, which would have been the normal procedure. In explaining the government's reaction to the Commission's work, Shivji asserts: 'what was anticipated was a report that would rationalise and legitimate the impending liberalisation of land in line with the policy diktat of the international financial institutions'.[43] The government therefore ignored the report and published a National Land Policy in June 1995.[44] Soon afterwards, the British Overseas Development Agency (later to become the Department for International Development) sponsored a technical legal consultant to draft a land bill based on the National Land Policy.[45]

The fact that the pattern of land reform has not been uniform in all areas and has not happened in a neat sequence across the continent should not be taken to mean that the main thrust of the changes is not remarkably similar everywhere. Africa's new land laws – whether they have already been passed, are under

45

consideration or will be on the books in the foreseeable future – will fundamentally alter land relations on the continent. The main thrust of the new land laws is to liberalize land tenure to enable land to be held individually rather than communally. The aim is to provide for and encourage foreign investment in land. Shivji has argued that the outcome of this process will be 'displacement and marginalisation'.[46] To take one example, the alienation of village land and of pastoral land[47] facilitated by Tanzania's Land Act 1998 will take place through the mechanism of certificates of investment that are designed to attract investors interested in the exploitation of the country's natural resources, including wildlife, animals, minerals and timber.[48] The relevant legal instrument is the National Investment (Promotion and Protection) Act 1990 which provides in section 26 that in cases where the Investment Promotion Centre grants a potential investor a certificate of approval, the Minister for Lands shall then be obliged to grant 'a lease of appropriate land for a term suited to the requirement of his enterprise'. The section also sets out that village land shall be leased for commercial activity only as a joint venture with the village government or its cooperative society. The mechanism of the joint venture suggests that equal protection and opportunities will be available to both parties, an idea that is to be doubted given the inequality of bargaining power and resources that are likely to characterize such relationships. In Shivji's view, what will occur will be the alienation of village land in the guise of joint ventures.[49] During the course of Tanzania's land reform debate, much of the pressure being exerted by foreign investors had its source in South African farmers who, looking northwards for investment opportunities and having been granted impressive land concessions in Mozambique, were targeting Tanzania as a business location.[50]

Conclusion

Network theory has been shown in Chapter 1 to be concerned with the ways the interests of diverse groups are translated, in this case into issues of land law reform. It can be seen that pressures to address the grievances of rural constituents did not come to play a significant role in the network or to find expression in it. Instead, what began as a process of demands by rural constituents that attention be paid to land issues ended in a vast overhaul of land laws which, far from addressing these concerns, actually threatens to worsen the situation of peasants, reducing their security of tenure and consolidating the privatization of land. The demands of rural constituents were lost in translation between the moment of their articulation as demands and the final stage of law-making.

This chapter has sought to explore the broad contours of Africa's land problems today and to suggest that, for the purported 'beneficiaries'[51] of land reform, these problems have not been addressed. Indeed, new land questions and significant new land conflicts can be seen to be emerging. In what follows, I explore aspects of the network of contemporary land law reform. I show how the demands of powerful actors have dominated the last two decades and set the terms of Africa's land reform debates. I ask: how is it that law came to play such a prominent role in land reform? And how might we explain why many countries went, seemingly inevitably, down the road of appointing commissions of inquiry into land matters, drafting new national land policies and passing new land laws?

Notes

1 Witness, for example, the support of the British government and the World Bank for the privatization of water in Tanzania, a process in which the British water firm Biwater, the Department for International Development (DfID) and the British consultancy firm Adam Smith International are involved. The World Development Movement estimates that £273,000 of the United Kingdom aid budget went to Adam Smith International for consultancy services that included the production of publicity material extolling the merits of the privatization including, infamously, a pro-water privatization video and song, the lyrics of which include the words 'Our old industries are dry like crops and privatization brings the rain'. For details, see <www.wdm.org.uk/news/presrel/current/biwatertanzan.htm> (accessed December 2005).

2 'The history of land reform is as long as the history of the world, extending back into medieval, ancient and biblical times.' (E. Tuma, *Twenty-Six Centuries of Agrarian Reform: A Comparative Analysis* [Berkeley: University of California Press, 1965], p. 3.)

3 United Nations, *Land Reforms: Defects in Agrarian Structure as Obstacles to Economic Development* (New York: United Nations, 1951), p. 89, cited in T. J. Byres, 'Introduction: Contextualizing and Interrogating the GKI Case for Redistributive Reform', *Journal of Agrarian Change*, 4 (1 & 2) (2004), pp. 1–16, 2.

4 Ibid., p. 2.

5 See *Our Common Interest: Report of the Commission for Africa* (London: Commission for Africa, 2005). The full report is also available at <www.commissionforafrica.org/english/home/newsstories.html> (accessed December 2005).

6 H. Bernstein, 'Land Reform: Taking a Long(er) View', *Journal of Agrarian Change*, 2 (4) (2002), pp. 433–63, 433.

7 See ibid.

8 C. D. Deere and M. Leon, 'Who Owns the Land? Gender and Land Titling Programmes in Latin America', *Journal of Agrarian Change*, 1 (3) (2001), pp. 440–67, 440–1.

9 Byres, 'Introduction: Contextualizing and Interrogating the GKI Case for Redistributive Reform', pp. 1–16.

10 S. Moyo, *The Land Question in Africa: Research Perspectives and Questions* (Dakar: CODESRIA Green Book, forthcoming).

11 B. de Sousa Santos, *Toward a New Legal Common Sense: Law, Globalization, and Emancipation* (London: Butterworths, 2002), p. 168.

12 Ibid.

13 Y. Vyas, K. K. Okech-Owiti and S. Wanjala (eds), *Law and Development in the Third World* (Nairobi: Faculty of Law, 1994).

14 See Byres, 'Introduction: Contextualizing and Interrogating the GKI Case for Redistributive Reform', pp. 1–16.

15 H. Bernstein, 'Land Reform', pp. 433–63.

16 See K. Griffin, A. R. Khan and A. Ickowitz, 'Poverty and Distribution of Land', *Journal of Agrarian Change*, 2 (3) (2002), pp. 279–330.

17 Based as it is at the School of Oriental and African Studies (SOAS), University of London. For an account of its early days, see T. J. Byres, 'The Peasants Seminar of the University of London, 1972–1989: A Memoir', *Journal of Agrarian Change*, 1 (3) (2001), pp. 343–88.

18 See Griffin, Khan and Ickowitz, 'Poverty and Distribution of Land'.

19 See Byres, 'Neo-Classical Neo-Populism Twenty-Five Years On: Déjà Vu and Déjà Passé', *Journal of Agrarian Change*, 4 (1 & 2) (2004), pp. 17–44.

20 See Bernstein, 'Land Reform' and J. Petras, 'Latin America: The Resurgence of the Left', *New Left Review*, 223 (1997), pp. 17–47. For a detailed account of the origins and historical context of Brazil's Movimiento Rural Sem Terra, its strategies and the obstacles it faces, see S. Banford and J. Rocha, *Cutting the Wire: The Story of the Landless Movement in Brazil* (London: Latin America Bureau, 2002).

21 A. Mafeje, 'The Agrarian Question in Southern Africa and Accumulation from Below', *SAPEM*, 10 (5) (1997), pp. 33–9.

22 H. Bernstein, 'Rural Land and Land Conflicts in Sub-Saharan Africa', in S. Moyo and P. Yeros (eds), *Reclaiming the Land: The Resurgence of Rural Movements in Africa, Asia and Latin America* (London: Zed Books, 2005), pp. 67–101.

23 M. Mamdani, 'Extreme but not Exceptional: Towards an Analysis of the Agrarian Question in Uganda', *Journal of Peasant Studies*, 14 (2), (1986), pp. 191–225.

24 Moyo, *The Land Question in Africa*, p. 1.

25 Ibid., p. 14.

26 S. Moyo, 'The Land Occupation Movement and Democratisation in Zimbabwe: Contradictions of Neo-Liberalism', *Millennium: Journal of International Studies*, 30 (2) (2001), pp. 311–30.

27 S. Moyo and P. Yeros, 'The Resurgence of Rural Movements under Neoliberalism', in Moyo and Yeros (eds), *Reclaiming the Land*, pp. 8–64.

28 P. Peters, 'Inequality and Social Conflict over Land in Africa', *Journal of Agrarian Change*, 4 (3) (2004), pp. 269–314.

29 C. Toulmin, 'The New Tragedy of the Commons', *New Internationalist* (special issue on Africa), 14 March 2005.

30 Moyo, *The Land Question in Africa*, p. 3.

31 Ibid.

32 See *The East African*, 30 August 2004. Available at <www.nationmedia.com/eastafrican/current/Regional/Regional300820042.html> (accessed December 2005)

33 See, for example, *Daily Nation*, 31 August 2004. Available at <www.nationmedia.com/dailynation/nmgcontententry.asp?category_id=1&newsid=14712> (accessed December 2005).

34 For an overview, see *A Summary of Land Policy Principles Drawn from the Commission of Inquiry into the Land Law System of Kenya* ('Njonjo Commission'), The Constitution of Kenya Review Commission (CKRC), Proceedings of the National Civil Society Conference on Land Reform and the Land Question. Available at <www.oxfam.org.uk/what_we_do/issues/livelihoods/landrights/downloads/kenyalanreformprocesses.doc> (accessed December 2005).

35 P. McAuslan, *Bringing the Law Back In: Essays in Land, Law and Development* (London: Ashgate, 2003), p. 248.

36 L. A. Wily, 'Land Tenure Reform and the Balance of Power in Eastern and Southern Africa', in Overseas Development Institute, *Natural Resource Perspectives*, 58 (June 2000), p. 2.

37 See Women's Land Rights in Southern and Eastern Africa, 'A Short Report on FAO/Oxfam GB Workshop held in Pretoria, South Africa, 17–19 June 2003'. Available at <www.oxfam.org.uk/what_we_do/ issues/livelihoods/landrights/africa_gen.htm> (accessed December 2005).

38 Although it must be remembered that the Tanzanians omitted one step in the sequence when the government failed to issue a White Paper responding to the findings of the Presidential Commission of Inquiry into Land Matters. This is discussed below.

39 Transcripts of the evidence heard by the Commission run to twenty volumes. There are, in addition, several hundred audio cassettes to be found on deposit with Tanzania National Archives and in the East African section of the University of Dar es Salaam library.

40 I. G. Shivji, *Not Yet Democracy: Reforming Land Tenure in Tanzania* (London: International Institute of Environment and Development, 1998).

41 United Republic of Tanzania Ministry of Land, Housing and Urban Development, *Report of the Presidential Commission of Inquiry into Land Matters* (Uppsala: Scandinavian Institute of African Studies, 1994). Volume 1 of the report is entitled *Land Policy and Land Tenure Structure* and Volume 2, *Selected Land Disputes and Recommendations*.

42 Ibid.

43 I. G. Shivji, 'Guest Editor's Introduction: Not Yet Uhuru', *Change*, 5 (1997), pp. 2–3.

44 See United Republic of Tanzania, *National Land Policy* (Dar es Salaam: Ministry of Lands, Housing and Urban Development, 1995). For a detailed discussion of the policy, see I. Juma, 'Problems of the National Land Policy', *Change*, 5 (1997), pp. 18–30.

45 P. McAuslan, *A Draft of the Bill for the Land Act* (Dar es Salaam: Ministry of Lands, Housing and Urban Development, 1996).

46 Shivji, *Not Yet Democracy*, p. 105.

47 J. T. Mwaikusa, 'The Policy Paper and Its Implications for Pastoral Lands', *Change*, 5 (1997); and I. G. Shivji and W. B. Kapinga, *Maasai Rights in Ngorongoro, Tanzania* (London: International Institute for Environment and Development, 1998).

48 Shivji, *Not Yet Democracy*.

49 Ibid.

50 Ibid.

51 M. Chossudovsky, '"Apartheid" Moves to Sub-Saharan Africa', *Third World Resurgence*, 76 (1996).

3 Paying for law: the World Bank and bilateral donors

Having explored the meaning of land reform in an era of neo-liberalism and discussed the vexed and long-running debate over the existence and possible nature of Africa's land questions, it is clear that the process of land reform has been characterized by an emphasis on law. This has entailed the drafting of national land policies, the appointment of commissions of inquiry into land issues and the enactment of new land laws, although the sequence and timing of events and the experience of addressing land tenure questions has often differed. In this chapter and in Chapter 4, I seek to explore further how and why contemporary land reform has come to mean a focus on land law reform. The observation that law has come to prominence in this field has been made by Patrick McAuslan in his important account of his own involvement in land reform. He has pointed to the existence in the present day of a 'commitment to developing a legal response to land reform, to seeing land reform as being, in part, land *law* reform'.[1] Similarly, he notes that 'land reform ... is itself increasingly presented as being a candidate for legal – that is, Western-type legal – solutions'[2] and that in the case, for example, of Tanzania, 'land reform is pre-eminently land law reform'.[3] Although these are insightful comments, I do not believe the reasons for the prominence of law are adequately explained by the author.[4] McAuslan's work as one of land reform's leading technical legal consultants and academic commentators is discussed in detail in Chapter 4 where the place of the 'law laboratory' in the land reform process is discussed. In this chapter, I wish to investigate the significant role that international financial institutions have played in the project to alter land tenure in Africa.

The first part of this chapter details the recent policy declarations emanating from the World Bank and shows why that institution, supported by bilateral aid donors, views the formalization of land relations to be central to development. The promotion of individual tenure and of formal rural credit markets goes hand in hand in the World Bank's vision. In the second part of this chapter, the way in which the World Bank and bilateral donors form part of a network of African land law is explored. I argue that through their funding of legal solutions to Africa's land problems as they have come to perceive them, the World Bank and bilateral donors have made themselves indispensable elements of this network.

Promoting the rule of law

If the last two decades have been the age of land law reform in Africa, this emphasis on the law must be placed in a broader political context. Since the end of the Cold War, a great deal of importance has been attached to promoting the rule of law. In Eastern Europe, South America, Asia and sub-Saharan Africa, the rule of law is seen as the cure for perceived economic and political ills. International financial institutions and bilateral donors have poured millions into what is referred to as 'rule of law aid' or 'rule of law reform'.[5] Estimates of the amount of assistance disbursed as rule of law aid vary: it is thought to have been US$ 500 million from multilateral development banks in the late 1990s[6] and US$ 9 billion from all development agencies and multilateral banks in the last decade.[7]

Carothers has provided a comprehensive definition of the rule of law as 'a system in which the laws are public knowledge, are clear in meaning, and apply equally to everyone'.[8] Spreading the rule of law by reforming laws (such as company laws) and legal institutions (such as the courts and the police) is seen as the necessary follow-up to the political and economic liberalization that has been imposed on the developing world since the late

1990s. It is perceived by its advocates to be relatively uncontentious, as a promotion of principles rather than profits.[9] Its intricate connection with capitalism is, however, inescapable. In the unusually explicit words of the director of Britain's Institute of Economic Affairs, 'what Africa needs is capitalism and its first cousin the rule of law'.[10]

There is a tension between viewing rule of law assistance as flowing naturally from, and being a necessary consolidation of, political and economic liberalization and asserting, as is common, that it does not constitute political interference in the domestic affairs of the member countries of international financial institutions. This contradiction is apparent in the World Bank's stated aims on technical legal assistance. The Bank's position on such funding is that it is important to 'ensure that its legal assistance projects are in accordance with its policy of non-interference in the politics of its member countries'.[11] However, the World Bank also holds that 'in the light of the close linkages between economic and legal reforms, it is important that any assistance to the borrowing countries' legal reforms should be part of the Bank's country assistance strategies that identify reform priorities in a range of areas'.[12] It is difficult to see how these two positions are reconcilable: the promotion of the rule of law is, as Carothers points out, an inherently political project.[13] In his recent account of working on land law reform as a technical legal consultant, Patrick McAuslan also alludes to these dual aims but does not offer any explanation of how their contradictions might be overcome.[14] I elaborate on this point in Chapter 4.

Seen in the context of a global project to promote the rule of law, African land law reform is but a component of an extensive economic and political project but it is arguable that land law reform is the most important such reform taking place on the continent.

53

The role of the World Bank in the privatization of land

Historical perspectives The World Bank has produced a series of influential reports on land matters since the 1970s and has been a key actor in setting the policy agenda on issues of land tenure. This has been pointed out by a number of commentators. Toulmin and Quan, for example, have argued that: 'Much of Africa remains heavily dependent on development assistance. As a consequence, African governments have been particularly subject to the ebb and flow of donor thinking about the importance of the land question and how it should be addressed.'[15]

Williams has also pointed out that 'for more than a decade and a half [since the last review of land issues in 1981] the World Bank's land policy greatly influenced the kind of development activity that was financed and supported throughout the world by donors and international financial institutions'.[16]

Throughout the 1980s, which marked the beginning of the serious debates on land reform that have bequeathed to Africa its most recent land laws, the Bank's emphasis was on issues of land titling and registration.[17] This formed part of the institution's structural adjustment agenda which, in emphasizing economic liberalization more generally, advocated the privatization of land and the promotion of land markets. It was thought that by abolishing customary tenure and instead formalizing land tenure regimes, as well as recommending and supporting land titling projects, farmers would be provided with the security of tenure and thus with the incentives they required to improve and invest in land.

In the 1990s, this thinking was modified to some extent as the Bank came to the view that in some circumstances customary tenure did not necessarily inhibit agricultural productivity.[18] It was argued that although land titling could provide incentives to farmers, this was only workable in countries in which market economies were more fully developed. This was not a radical break from its previous position in that the Bank continued to hold to the idea that formalization and titling of land rights was ultimately the most desirable goal. It was rather recognition that this could not be achieved with immediate effect in all situations. In relation to Africa, the Bank therefore modified its position on titling, asserting that over time the 'market economy ... will eventually produce a land tenure system that, while not identical, will bear strong resemblance to the western concept of ownership'[19] and that it was at this point that interventions should take place to register tenure changes.

Recent policy declarations Having embraced the idea that the transition from communal to private land tenure is inevitable over time, the World Bank can be seen more recently to have turned its attention to what may lie beyond this development in land relations. If the first phase of the World Bank's engagement in land issues in Africa in the 1980s and 1990s was concerned with the privatization of land tenure, interest has subsequently turned to what might be described as the potential scope for financializing land relations. While land disputes, difficulties of access to land, widespread dispossession and land grabbing continued apace at the national level, attention at the international level was thus already beginning to turn to the role which land might play on the wider macroeconomic plane by promoting economic growth and good governance. As in the past, the World Bank has taken a lead in setting the policy agenda. In order to demonstrate the concerns of this current phase of the World Bank's involvement in land issues, the most recent policy document to be issued by the World Bank is discussed.

In 2002 the World Bank issued for the purposes of consultation two drafts of a Policy Research Report on land issues which set out the Bank's thinking on a range of issues such as land reform, land administration, customary tenure, land markets and formal rural credit. The first draft report was entitled *Land Institutions and Land Policy* and the second *Land Policy for Pro-Poor Development*.[20]

In 2003 the Bank then published the final Policy Research Report under the title *Policy Research Report: Land Policies for Growth and Poverty Reduction*.[21] The Policy Research Report was a project of the World Bank's Research Department and was presented as the culmination of a process of review spanning two years and as a review by the Bank of its global involvement in lending in the land sector. The last such review was carried out in 1981. In 2001, the World Bank had completed what it described as a 'lessons learned' study that formed the basis of an electronic consultation that year.[22] The first draft of the Policy Research Report was then produced with the collaboration of multilateral and bilateral organizations such as the UK's Department for International Development (DfID), Germany's Gesellschaft für technische Zusammenarbeit (GTZ) and the United States Agency for International Development (USAID). It is significant that the report took the form of a Policy Research Report. These are the most important vehicles which the Bank's researchers can employ to attempt to influence thinking on a particular issue from within the institution and are widely thought to be influential documents, especially as they are generally produced at a rate of only one a year.

Despite the attempts of the World Bank to appear to consult with civil society groups and interested parties on the implications of its evolving land policy, very few individuals or groups were able to acquire, comment upon or challenge the fundamental assumptions upon which the drafts are based. Indeed, as I noted in Chapter 1, the World Bank was severely criticized by a number of civil society groups for failing to consult to any meaningful extent on drafts of the Policy Research Report. Criticisms which were levelled at the Bank included: reliance on a small number of experts, failure to invite civil society groups to attend workshops, exclusion of landless peoples, failure to circulate the drafts to interested parties, over-reliance on the internet, and imposing severe timeframes on the process of consultation.[23] Nevertheless, the report identifies agreed key principles and will form the basis for coordinating the Bank's approach to land issues in the future. Given the influence exerted by previous publications of World Bank policy, there is good reason to suggest that the current Policy Research Report will determine the land agenda for some time to come.

On the evidence of the Policy Research Report, the World Bank's current approach to land relations is based on the idea that the ways in which land rights are defined is of central importance to economic growth, to the effective use of land as a resource, to efforts at poverty reduction and to good governance.[24] The report is premised on the belief that the way in which property rights are assigned has important implications for efficiency and economic growth in rural areas.[25] The report identifies four issues which can have an adverse affect on land-related and general economic growth in rural areas. First, in terms of production outcomes, the World Bank asserts that to the extent that owner-operated farms are more efficient than wage-labour-operated farms, the distribution of land as between these types of farms is important. Second, it asserts that secure land tenure is essential in order to provide investment incentives both at the level of the household and of the economy. Third, the frequency of disputes and situations of insecure tenure are seen as disincentives to invest in land and thus as undermining the entire rural economy by discouraging domestic and foreign investment in both land and related non-agricultural ventures. Fourth, the inability to use land as collateral for accessing credit is perceived to have far-reaching effects on households in terms of their ability to make indivisible investments. It also inhibits the emergence and efficiency of rural credit and other factor markets.[26] The report points out that, 'taken together, the impact of land-related restrictions on economic growth can be very large' and provides as an example the case of India where 'land market distortions' are said to be responsible for a 1.3 percentage point reduction in economic growth a year.[27]

Paying for law

Arguably the most important aspect of the report is its promotion of the idea of rural credit markets. According to the Bank, land does more than simply provide a shelter and a means of livelihood; it is also the 'main vehicle to invest, accumulate wealth, and transfer it between generations'.[28] Access to land affects incentives to make investments and the ability of the poor to access financial markets. Thus, land is fundamental not just to poverty reduction but also to economic growth. Policies that make it possible to use land as a means to access credit turn it from a dead asset into an economically viable resource, resulting in what the World Bank portrays as major equity benefits. The ability of households to access credit using their land as collateral has widespread implications on two levels according to the World Bank. First, it affects a household's ability to make indivisible investments and, second, it affects the emergence and workings of rural credit markets. From this perspective, economic growth as a whole is held back if rural land is allowed to remain a dead asset.

The acquisition of secure tenure rights not only increases investment in land, for example in the form of labour inputs, it is also seen as increasing the supply of credit from formal credit institutions using land as collateral. The World Bank suggests that the development of credit markets is a good thing in its own right but emphasizes that the characteristics of the credit market are also relevant. A credit market that demands high transactions costs for lending excludes small farmers, meaning that the benefits of borrowing and more widely of titling accrue only to medium and large farms. The close relationship between titling and access to credit is central to the report.[29]

In recent years, as I have noted above, it appears that the World Bank has been prepared to countenance the idea that titling is only one way to achieve its goal of increased investment and productivity.[30] The report thus set out that the high costs associated with titling mean it is only worth carrying it out where informal credit transactions are already taking place or a formal credit market that accepts the use of land as collateral is already in existence or where potentially profitable investment opportunities are available. In conditions that fall short of this, lower precision is needed in tenure regimes so that group rights, for example, might suffice. In the view of the Bank, as less than ideal tenure arrangements (that is, anything short of formal individual title) evolve, they will in time provide opportunities for the development of credit markets.[31]

Although it admits the empirical evidence to support it is scant, the Bank believes that the ability to use land as collateral for raising credit and the existence of a well-developed land sales market could enhance social mobility and urban–rural migration. The emergence of financial markets to support markets in land is seen as having a beneficial impact on the broader rural economy by raising funds for both agricultural and non-agricultural activities, by providing working capital and by facilitating access to credit as insurance. Incomplete credit markets are thus seen as imperfections in wider markets. The Bank's overall advocacy of rural credit markets is summed up in the suggestion that without them 'poor people would fail to get out of poverty not because they are unproductive or lack skills, but because, due to credit market imperfections, they never get the opportunity to utilise their innate ability'.[32]

The second important aspect of the report, and one that, it should be pointed out, has serious implications for gender relations, is its approach to agricultural labour. It is clear from the Policy Research Report that the availability of family labour, which was described in the first draft of the report as 'non-contractible effort' – although this labelling was quietly dropped in subsequent drafts and in the final published report[33] – is considered to be a crucial factor in boosting agricultural productivity. The Bank points out that owner-operated farms tend to have a competitive advantage over those that are reliant on waged labour. That this is due in large part to the fact that family labour tends to be unwaged is not mentioned. Instead, the competitive advantage of small farms, it is suggested, derives from the fact that their owner-operators do not incur the costs associated with supervising contracted labour.

The report cites two specific circumstances in which it is believed that owner-operated farms are more efficient than those dependent on waged labour. Where agricultural land is held in fragmented plots or at some distance to the residence, as is often the case, and where farmers need to be able adapt to microvariations in the weather, owner-operated holdings are more efficient. Although it does not set out explicitly why this is thought to be the case, it can be deduced that unwaged labour does not incur costs for time wasted travelling between plots or while waiting for improvements in the weather. Because family labour is not paid and because it is assumed that it can find other productive tasks to fill time between working on agricultural land, it is to be preferred to wage labour in these circumstances. According to the World Bank, the availability of flexible labour can have profound and important production outcomes and, in this way, affect the efficiency of small owner-operated units.

For the World Bank, in addition to the efficiency impact of owner-operated farms, the productivity advantages that accrue to owner-operators will also have important consequences for equity. The report envisages that the natural functioning of land markets will ensure that transfers of land take place between large and small farmers. This is due to the fact that the productivity advantages of small farmers – their access to highly motivated family labour, low supervision costs and strong supervision skills – will dictate that larger farmers are less efficient and therefore less desirable. This will result in land sales by larger farmers to smaller ones. Overall, this is perceived to be an equitable and important outcome.

A further notable feature of the Policy Research Report is that it links land policy and poverty reduction, explicitly mentioning the problems entailed in household defaulting on rural loans:

> at low levels of income and in the absence of other mechanisms for social security, land serves as a social safety net. Foreclosing on the land of households who have defaulted on credit would deprive them of the basic means of livelihood and may not be socially desirable which is essentially the reason for customary systems restricting the marketability of land.[34]

Although the language of poverty reduction was apparent as early as the first draft report, it was subsequently made more central to the policy document. Indeed, it is notable that the final published report came to incorporate the idea of poverty reduction in its title.

While the World Bank report does acknowledge that the extent to which land markets should be promoted has recently been a contested issue in Africa, it may be inferred from its strong advocacy of land markets and the supporting institutions of rural credit that it will be promoting such arrangements on the continent in the near future. Although formal rural credit institutions are developing relatively slowly in Africa and greater priority is clearly being attached to their development elsewhere in the world, the prominence in development thinking of evolutionary models which assume that 'land holding systems are evolving into individualised systems of ownership with greater market integration'[35] suggests that the Policy Research Report presents to Africa a vision of its own future. This has implications not just for the alienation of land to credit institutions but also, due to the use of family labour advocated by the Bank, for the social and economic position of women who labour on the land, an issue I take up in Chapter 6. The promotion of land markets threatens to create a class of indebted rural inhabitants whose alienation from their sole productive resource is attributable to their position as holders of dead capital that the World Bank wishes to see converted to productive economic assets.

The role of bilateral donors

Bilateral donors have played a central role in promoting, supporting and funding the drafting of new land laws in much of Africa. As already noted, bilateral donors such as the UK's DfID, Germany's GTZ and USAID were closely involved in the development of the World Bank's Policy Research Report. They participated in the consultation process surrounding the policy document and were involved in its formulation. In their lending practices they, like the World Bank, have also increasingly cast their attention beyond the privatization of land towards what I have described as its financialization. Adopting the language of poverty reduction, international aid donors now explicitly link property rights and economic growth. The emphasis is on land's potential as collateral. Formal rural credit markets are a seen as a necessary aspect of, and a means to bolster, the move away from communal tenure towards privatized land holding.

In 2004, the creation of the Commission for a Strong and Prosperous Africa, chaired by the British Prime Minister Tony Blair and widely known as the 'Blair Commission for Africa', provided an opportunity for land reform to be discussed as a development issue to which all international donors needed to turn their attention. By this time Geoff Mulgan, head of Downing Street's policy unit, had facilitated a visit to Britain by de Soto.[36] The latter's ideas had clearly influenced the thinking of the Blair government. This is evident from the report of the Blair Commission for Africa which is suffused with de Soto's perspectives on the importance of land to economic development and which vigorously supports the formalization of land reform.

There were concerted attempts to influence the Commission's thinking in relation to land issues in advance of the publication of its report, spearheaded by the International Institute for Environment and Development (IIED), the Natural Resources Institute (NRI) at the University of Greenwich and the Royal Africa Institute which jointly hosted an international conference in London at the end of 2004. The conference was attended by a number of African Ministers of Land and by members of the Blair Commission for Africa, such as the prominent Tanzanian academic and feminist activist Anna Tibaijuka. Although the Blair Commission's final report does address land issues, as I discuss below, subsequent statements from the IIED suggest that there was some disappointment about the extent of its engagement and what has been described as its lack of commitment to tackling land problems as an aspect of poverty reduction.[37]

The Commission refers to the importance of land throughout its report. In doing so, however, it makes an explicit connection between property rights and economic growth, thereby displaying its debt to the World Bank's Policy Research Report on the one hand and to de Soto's work on the other. The importance of the Blair Commission's report lies in its attempt to influence the international aid agenda and the policies of other donor countries. It does not confine itself to elaborating a development role for Britain alone but instead refers readily to the importance of all donor countries embracing the project to formalize land tenure, arguing that: 'Land reform is an intensely political issue in Africa and many donor countries have pulled back from addressing it in recent decades.'[38] Britain is thus evidently seeking to put itself at the forefront of bilateral aid policy in relation to land.

For the Blair Commission on Africa, access to land and access to collateral are intricately linked. The Commission's insistence that 'African governments must take measures to give poor people, particularly women, access to land and secure rights to their land'[39] would not displease many people in Africa who have known landlessness and long-running insecurity of tenure, as evidenced by the report of the Presidential Commission of Inquiry into Land Matters in Tanzania discussed in Chapter 2. However, the Blair Commission strongly suggests that the uses of land go beyond providing shelter and a source of livelihood. It echoes the World Bank and de Soto in stating: 'When people have title to their land they feel more confident about investing and also can use the title deeds as security to obtain loans.'[40] The demand for 'security' voiced by rural and many urban inhabitants such as slum dwellers is lost in the project to financialize African land relations, in which the notion of security is equated with collateral: the security not of the home or of the farm owner but of the commercial lender.

According to the Blair Commission report, it is essential to promote the growth of small and medium enterprises (SMEs) in order to ensure poverty reduction and 'release Africa's entrepreneurial energies'.[41] Just as the very imagery employed by de Soto and the World Bank finds its way into the Blair Commission's report, so too does a neo-populist approach to the family farm. We are told that 'the most important SMEs in Africa are the family farms'[42] and it is therefore important that a suitable investment climate is developed 'in which Africa's farmers ... are ready to improve their own land'.[43] The following account sums up the report's approach:

> small entrepreneurs suffer most from a poor investment climate. Access to credit and other financial services is important to growth and investment, yet few small businesses or individuals are able to get the access they need. This partly reflects a lack of access to property rights for the majority of poor people: formal legal title to homes and land are often required as collateral to obtain commercial credit. More generally, effectively enforced property rights are important for reducing investment costs and risks.[44]

Two observations can be made concerning this passage. The first is that it confirms that the small family farm should be viewed as a small business, while suggesting that collateral secured on land might also be employed for non-farm enterprises, an approach adopted and strongly advocated by the World Bank. Second, the passage displays an overriding concern with improved investment climates, enforceable rights and controlled investment costs and risks. These demands are a far cry from the calls for security of tenure and access to land of Africa's rural constituents. They are directed instead at the commercial sector and specifically at commercial lenders who have been entrusted with the development of formal rural credit markets. Economic growth, not poverty reduction, is the true objective of the Blair Commission. Although it asserts that poverty reduction is to be achieved through economic growth, it wilfully ignores the risks involved for the poor in credit markets. It is silent on repossession, on exposure to risk in the face of uncertain and fluctuating agricultural markets or of the increased family labour that may have to be commandeered to pay back commercial loans. The role of law is also clearly stated: alongside 'strengthening the assets of the poor' to enable them 'to participate more effectively in markets', the report confirms that 'the economic, legal and governance environments shape the opportunities open to them'.[45]

Linking the global and the local

I argued in Chapter 1 that the creation of a network of African land reform would necessarily entail identifying the pertinent cause of the 'development problem' faced by African societies. This diagnostic role has been played by the World Bank which, from its location at the global level, has propagated the following message to the third world: if you have lacked development, it is because you lack the rule of law which brings with it the formalization of property. Dead capital is tied up in your land that can only be liberated by formalizing tenure relations.

Recent policy declarations by bilateral donors suggest that this diagnosis currently has widespread purchase. The World Bank has designated informal land tenure as the cause of underdevelopment and, in its customary evolutionary mode of thinking, believes that the transition from informal, communal tenure to formalized individual landholding will solve the perceived ills of the third world. This view of land relations has made what I would describe as the 'land law laboratory' attractive to international financial institutions. In Chapter 4, I will show how the personnel of the land law laboratory, technical legal consultants, have come to translate the interests of significant groups in the land reform process into issues of law and thus to play a central role in the network of African land reform. Prior to that, however, it is necessary to explore in greater depth the functioning of a discrete section of the network of African land reform, that is, the part constituted at the global level by the World Bank and bilateral donors.

In seeking to understand how land reform has come to mean land law reform, network theory enables us to explore how law has become an 'obligatory point of passage'[46] for those, such as international financial institutions, who are concerned with land matters. This allows us to recover a sense of agency that is often missing from standard accounts of land reform which have conveyed a sense of inevitability about the process: law is treated as the natural and sole means by which to address land problems.[47] Demonstrating the working of agency is not in itself sufficient, however. It is also important to be attentive to the economic and political context within which land reform has been played out since the early 1990s. As I showed in Chapter 2, the pressures faced by African governments on this issue were substantial: rural constituents demanded that problems of landlessness and the chaos and uncertainty caused by insecure tenure and overlapping claims to land be resolved. In the case of many African countries, such as Tanzania and Uganda, barely had calls to address land problems been heard than new land laws found their way on to the statute books. The land laws that have resulted, however, far from ensuring security of tenure and guarding against alienation of land and landlessness, have made these outcomes more likely. In relation to the Tanzanian Land Act 1998, for example, Shivji has said that it is 'geared to facilitate the alienation of village land, including pastoral lands ... it is not difficult to foresee that the immediate agrarian and other investors who would be given these lands under ... the certificate of investment, will be those interested in the rapid exploitation of natural resources'.[48] The purpose of the discussion that follows is to explore this perverse result.

As I have already noted, Kennedy has made the important observation that we need to be alert to the 'difficult distributional choices' entailed in land reform.[49] The need to study why one path is chosen rather than another is nowhere more important than in discussions of land reform. We need to ask why land reform is perceived as an area ripe for legal solutions. How is it that the path of land reform being pursued today is one that seeks to promote individual over communal tenure, rather than one aiming to strengthen communal relations[50] or to achieve land redistribution?[51]

In order to understand 'self-styled "new wave" agrarian reform in the age of neo-liberalism',[52] it is important to study law's role in the process. Here, Cutler's account of the function of law in neo-liberal globalization is particularly useful.[53] Cutler has noted that law links global and local political and economic orders in complex ways, forming what she describes as 'a juridical link between local and global political-legal orders'.[54] In Chapter 2, I described the impetus for land reform at local level, that is, the level of the nation-state. The focus of this chapter is on the global level occupied by international financial institutions and bilateral aid donors in the developed world. What links the local order of the nation-state with this global order is the law. For Cutler, law plays a crucial role in the globalization of capitalism in two interrelated ways. The first of these is by promoting certain values that are embodied in legal rules. Second, the law also has a cultural effect because it enforces the internalization of the disciplines necessary for the efficient operation of a neo-liberal political and economic order.

In Cutler's assessment, the law that is globalized has a specific nature as American or Anglo-American law. It has as its central purpose the promotion of neo-liberalism. Cutler reminds us of the importance of investigating the values that legal rules express and of being alert to their role in the private appropriation of surplus value. This analysis of the globalization of law's values can be usefully illustrated by reference to the detailed provisions contained in the Tanzania Land Act 1998.[55] There are two distinct issues to be investigated here. First, it is necessary to assess the law as it is contained in the Land Act 1998 and to determine the values expressed. How do these rules contribute to the private appropriation of capital? Second, what is the process by which these rules, and the values they embody, are globalized?

As will be clear from the discussion contained in Chapter 2, fierce debates surrounded the drafting and enactment of the Tanzania Land Act 1998 and controversy and disagreement over the purpose and direction of land reform marked that country more than most. The Land Act 1998 and the Village Land Act 1998 steered a very different course to that recommended by the Shivji Commission based on its extensive consultation across the country. It is clear the legislation had as its objective the creation of a suitable environment for investment in land by large-scale foreign buyers and the setting up of an efficient system for a market in land. The effect of these legal rules, to return to Cutler's analytical framework, will be to set the groundwork for the globalization of capitalism. The values promoted by the legislation are those of the market, private investment and the appropriation of surplus value.

An assessment of legal values need not be restricted solely to a consideration of relevant land laws, however. Surrounding legislation also operates to create suitable economic conditions. In Tanzania, the National Investment (Promotion and Protection) Act 1990 provides in section 26 that when an investor is granted a certificate of approval by the Investment Promotion Centre, the body in charge of attracting investors to the country and facilitating their business, the Minister responsible for land 'shall grant him on such terms and conditions as may be prescribed a lease of appropriate land for a term suited to the requirement of his enterprise'. The Act goes on: 'Provided that land belonging to any registered village shall not be leased for commercial activities other than joint ventures with the village government or the village's co-operative society, save that such land may be sub-leased by the village itself for small or medium-scale public or private economic activities. Any lease granted under this section shall be for a term not exceeding 99 years.' Shivji has argued that this section of the Act will facilitate little more than wholesale alienation of land under the guise of joint ventures.[56] The implications for women and for others excluded from the village government structures mentioned in the Act are equally clear: a male-dominated peasant elite is capable of entering into agreements with investors to the disadvantage of many members of the village.

The second important aspect of the law that deserves attention is, for Cutler, its cultural effect. The process of globalizing law 'is integral to the internalisation of neo-liberal discipline by elites' while also ensuring that this discipline is in turn reproduced in local laws as well as transnational laws.[57] Cutler argues that 'globalised law advances the interests of a transnational class whose members function as the "organic intellectuals" for the globalisation of capitalism'[58] and that a transnational class 'advances a particular legal culture informed by neo-liberal values and the privileging of private ordering as the most natural, efficient, consensual and just means of regulating commercial and productive relations'.[59]

The global land reform network

How might Cutler's characterization of law assist in understanding the functioning of a network of African land law reform?

First, Cutler's theoretical approach allows us to model the different levels at which land law reform has been debated and enacted. Law forms the link between the many levels of land law reform, starting at the global level with international financial institutions and moving through national governments down to peasants in the fields. The notion of a 'juridical link' allows us to see the phenomenon of land law reform in its global and local aspects. It also enables us to recognize that the network of land law reform is not created and carefully maintained for its own sake. The globalization of law, as Cutler reminds us, is fundamental to the globalization of capitalism. Harnessing this to Latour's network theory allows us to look inside the 'law laboratory' and to question why certain diagnoses are reached and certain solutions recommended. The diagnosis that the problems of economic development lie in non-formalized land relations can only take place in the context of neo-liberalism, and the solution – that land relations must be formalized – likewise has its political and economic context.

Cutler further urges us to be alert to the ways in which the globalization of law promotes certain values. The replacement of communal tenure with private tenure is achieved by the spread of a land law network or, put otherwise, by the globalization of law. Across Africa, remarkably similar new land laws will seek to replace complex and varied forms of communal tenure with private land tenure. Whereas network theory provides a powerful account of how individuals might work to create and sustain the network which achieves this alteration in land relations, Cutler's attention to the role of elites goes further to explain the endurance of networks. Local elites internalize the globalization of law, naturalizing and privileging private ordering and portraying the process of its triumph over other forms of social and economic life, such as communal tenure, as consensual. In accounting for the role of a transnational elite, the members of which act as 'organic intellectuals for the globalisation of capitalism',[60]

Cutler's account allows us to explore the role of powerful actors in the land reform process.

The network thus created should not, however, be thought to fall into disuse or disrepair when the task of drafting new, liberalizing property laws has been achieved. There are at least two ways such a network might be sustained over time. The first is through the follow-up work that appears to become necessary when the complex business of implementing new land laws is confronted. I discuss the difficulties surrounding implementation in Chapter 6 but the following example illustrates how the long-drawn-out process of passing and then implementing a new law can prolong the network of reform. In Uganda, the beginning of the process of land tenure reform can be traced to 1992 (if a number of unsuccessful or stalled attempts to address Ugandan land and agricultural issues by the World Bank, USAID, the University of Wisconsin Land Tenure Center and the Agricultural Secretariat of the Bank of Uganda are ignored) when a review of the constitution took place. In Article 237 it was stipulated that the Ugandan Parliament would enact a new land law within two years of its first sitting. In the aftermath of the passing of the Land Act 1998, it became evident that there would be major difficulties involved in implementing the new law.[61] The Ugandan government approached Britain's DfID for assistance with this stage of the process, leading to the setting up of a project called 'Securing Sustainable Livelihoods Through Land Tenure Reform' which was widely described as the Land Act Implementation Project.[62] This funded study involved a number of individuals who had originally been involved in advising on and drafting the new land law, including the original technical legal consultant.[63] It lasted fifteen months. Such subsequent work on the implementation of often enormously complex and detailed new land laws guarantees the continued relevance of the original network of land law reform and guarantees that the network will persist into the future.

The second way in which the network is sustained and continued is illustrated by an episode that arose after the passing into law of the Tanzania Land Act 1998 and Village Land Act 1998. In that instance, the new land laws were approved by Parliament in 1998 having been drafted by a British technical legal consultant, funded once again by DfID.[64] Following this, a large South African commercial bank sought to purchase a smaller Tanzanian bank but expressed anxiety about a clause on foreclosure contained in the new land legislation. In communications with the World Bank, they argued that the provision increased the risk of lending by requiring the courts to approve the foreclosure of mortgages in certain circumstances. This query was in turn raised by the World Bank in communications with DfID. At the request of the former, advice on the matter was sought from the technical legal consultant who had originally been responsible for drafting the law. He was able to reassure the South African investors about the workings of the Tanzanian Land Act and the sale went ahead.[65] The episode provides evidence that the network of African land law reform does not function solely during the relatively short-lived process of drafting land laws to facilitate privatization. It is required to remain in place. The long narrow network must then underpin private foreign investment, not just in land but also more widely in lucrative elements of the economy such as the commercial banking sector. The need of foreign investors for reassurance guarantees the continued function, relevance and importance of a recently created network. This longer-term perspective is summed up by McAuslan in the following passage:

> It is essential that the reforms, once introduced, are carefully monitored, so that adjustments may be made as and when needed. At the end of the day, while land reform might, just, still be the preserve of the lawyer, the products of that reform – the new land laws – are the property of the nation and the nation must be assisted in embracing and working within those new laws.[66]

Conclusion

This chapter has sought to explore a discrete section of the network of African land law reform. It has discussed the role of the World Bank and bilateral donors in promoting legal solutions to problems of land and shown how the global and the local are connected through a 'juridical link'.[67] The ways in which law is globalized, the values embodied in this globalized law and its cultural effects have been explored.

I now move on to investigate the role of technical legal consultants in the process of land law reform. Focusing on a further section of the network of African land reform which I characterize as the 'law laboratory', I seek to link the programmes of international financial institutions and bilateral donors discussed in this chapter with the work of technical legal consultants responsible for drafting new land laws.

Notes

1 P. McAuslan, *Bringing the Law Back In: Essays in Land, Law and Development* (London: Ashgate, 2003), p. 248 (author's italics).

2 Ibid., p. 245.

3 Ibid., p. 249.

4 See A. Manji, 'Cause and Consequence in Law and Development: Review of Patrick McAuslan's *Bringing the Law Back In*', *Journal of Modern African Studies*, 43 (1) (2005), pp. 119–38.

5 T. Carothers, 'The Rule of Law Revival', *Foreign Affairs*, 77 (2) (1998), pp. 95–106.

6 P. Messick, 'Judicial Reform and Economic Development: A Survey of the Issues', *World Bank Observer*, 14 (1999).

7 D. Trubek, 'Rule of Law Projects, Yesterday, Today and Tomorrow', Lecture presented at Harvard Law School, 2003.

8 Carothers, 'The Rule of Law Revival'.

9 Ibid.

10 See <www.iea.org.uk/record.jsp?type=news&ID=203> (accessed December 2005).

11 World Bank, *The World Bank and Technical Legal Assistance*, PRWP 414 (Washington, DC: World Bank, 1995), p. 5. See also the long-running debate about the relationship between Article IV, section 10 of the World Bank's Articles of Agreement and its lending decisions relat-

ing to development and human rights. Article IV, section 10 states: 'The Bank and its officers shall not interfere in the political affairs of any member; nor shall they be influenced in their decisions by the political character of the member or members concerned. Only economic considerations shall be relevant to their decisions, and these considerations shall be weighed impartially.' There has been much discussion on the implications of this provision for the Bank's work. See I. Shihata, 'The World Bank and Human Rights', in International Commission of Jurists, *Report of a Regional Seminar on Economic, Social and Cultural Rights* (Abidjan, 1998); and more generally the excerpts contained in H. Steiner and P. Alston, *International Human Rights in Context: Text and Materials* (Oxford: Oxford University Press, 2000), pp. 1334–40.

12 World Bank, *The World Bank and Technical Legal Assistance*, p. 5.

13 Carothers, 'The Rule of Law Revival'.

14 McAuslan, *Bringing the Law Back In*.

15 C. Toulmin and J. Quan, 'Evolving Land Rights, Tenure and Policy in Sub-Saharan Africa', in C. Toulmin and J. Quan (eds), *Evolving Land Rights, Policy and Tenure in Africa* (London: International Institute for Environment and Development, 2000), pp. 1–29, 3.

16 S. Williams, *Report on Regional Workshop on Land Issues in Africa* 2002 (on file with the author).

17 World Bank, *Sub-Saharan Africa: From Crisis to Sustainable Growth* (Washington, DC: World Bank, 1989); J.-P. Platteau, *Land Reform and Structural Adjustment in Sub-Saharan Africa: Controversies and Guidelines* (Rome: Food and Agricultural Organization, 1992).

18 J. W. Bruce and S. E. Migot-Adholla, *Searching for Land Tenure Security in Africa* (Iowa: Kendall Hunt, 1994); K. Deininger and H. Binswanger, 'The Evolution of the World Bank's Land Policy: Principles, Experiences and Future Challenges', *World Bank Research Observer*, 14 (1999), pp. 247–76; T. C. Pinckey and P. K. Kimuyi,'Land Tenure Reform in East Africa: Good, Bad or Unimportant', *Journal of African Economies*, 3 (1) (1994), pp. 1–28.

19 Bruce and Migot-Adholla, *Searching for Land Tenure Security in Africa*.

20 The first draft was presented by Klaus Deininger, Chief Economist at the World Bank's Research Department, at the World Bank Regional Workshop on Land Issues in Africa, held in Kampala, Uganda, 29 April to 2 May 2002. See K. Deininger and G. Feder, 'Land Institutions and Policy: Some Key Messages of the Policy Research Report'. Available at <Inweb18.Worldbank.org/ESSD/essdext ... nsf/25ByDocname/ KdeiningerGFederPaper/$File/PRR_Enlish.pdf> (accessed December 2005).

21 World Bank, *Policy Research Report: Land Policies for Growth and Poverty Reduction* (Oxford: Oxford University Press, 2003).

22 World Bank, 'Electronic Conference on Land Policy and Sustainable Development' (2001). For details, see <www.oxfam.org. uk/landrights/Donormtg.rtf> (accessed December 2005).

23 See chapter 1 for details.

24 World Bank, *Policy Research Report: Land Policies for Growth and Poverty Reduction.*

25 Ibid., pp. xvii–xlvi.

26 Ibid.

27 Ibid.

28 Ibid., pp. xix–xx.

29 Ibid., pp. 17–22.

30 J. Quan, 'Land Tenure, Economic Growth and Poverty in Sub-Saharan Africa', in Toulmin and Quan (eds), *Evolving Land Rights*, pp. 31–49.

31 World Bank, *Policy Research Report: Land Policies for Growth and Poverty Reduction.*

32 Ibid.

33 The author was not a participant in the formal consultation process conducted by the World Bank at any stage. She did, however, analyse the first draft report for its gender implications. This work was carried out independently and her comments made available to Klaus Deininger, Chief Economist, World Bank Research Department. See A. Manji, 'The World Bank's Review of Land Policies: A Gender Analysis'. Available at <wwwInweb18.worldbank.org/ESSD/essdext. nsf/24DocByUnid/70432684716CDA4785256C87005B99ED/$FILE/ draft_prr.pdf> (accessed December 2005). This analysis drew attention to the relevance of the term 'non-contractible labour' and although the phrase itself was not used in subsequent drafts, the idea it encapsulates continues to inform the Bank in its approach to agricultural labour. For a more detailed discussion, see Chapter 6 below.

34 World Bank, *Policy Research Report: Land Policies for Growth and Poverty Reduction.*

35 I. Yngstrom, 'Women, Wives and Land Rights in Africa: Situating Gender Beyond the Household in the Debate Over Land Policy and Changing Tenure Systems', *Oxford Development Studies*, 30 (2002), pp. 21–40.

36 See 'Fine Words, Flawed Idea', *Guardian*, 11 September 2000. Available at <www.guardian.co.uk/Archive/Article/0,4273,4061838,00. html> (accessed December 2005).

37 C. Toulmin, 'The New Tragedy of the Commons', *New Internationalist* (Special Issue on Africa), 14 March 2005.

38 See *Our Common Interest: Report of the Commission for Africa* (London: Commission for Africa, 2005), p. 52. Available at <www.

Paying for law

commissionforafrica.org/english/home/newsstories.html> (accessed December 2005).

39 Ibid.

40 Ibid.

41 Ibid., p. 88.

42 Ibid., p. 89.

43 Ibid.

44 Ibid., p. 233.

45 Ibid., p. 225.

46 B. Latour, 'Give Me a Laboratory and I Will Raise the World', in K. D. Knorr-Cetina and M. Mulkay (eds), *Science Observed: Perspectives in the Social Study of Science* (London: Sage, 1983).

47 Manji, 'Cause and Consequence'.

48 I. G. Shivji, *Not Yet Democracy: Reforming Land Tenure in Tanzania* (London: International Institute for Environment and Development, 1998), p. 105. The workings of Tanzania's Certificates of Investment are discussed in Chapter 2.

49 D. Kennedy, 'Laws and Developments', in A. Perry and J. Hatchard (eds), *Law and Development: Facing Complexity in the 21st Century* (London: Cavendish, 2003), pp. 17–35.

50 R. Home, 'Outside de Soto's Bell Jar: Colonial/Postcolonial Law and the Exclusion of the Peri-Urban Poor', in R. Home and H. Lim, *Demystifying the Mystery of Capital: Land Tenure and Poverty in Africa and the Caribbean* (London: Glasshouse Press, 2004), pp. 11–30.

51 H. Bernstein, 'Land Reform: Taking a Long(er) View', *Journal of Agrarian Change*, 1 (2002), pp. 433–63.

52 Ibid., p. 433.

53 A. C. Cutler, 'Historical Materialism, Globalization, and Law: Competing Conceptions of Property', in M. Rupert and H. Smith (eds), *Historical Materialism and Globalization* (London: Routledge 2002), pp. 230–56.

54 Ibid., p. 230.

55 For a detailed discussion of the debates over methodology that characterized the debate on the Tanzania's land legislation, see A. Manji, 'Gender and the Politics of the Land Reform Process in Tanzania', *Journal of Modern African Studies*, 36 (4) (1998), pp. 645–67.

56 Shivji, *Not Yet Democracy*, p. 33.

57 Cutler, 'Historical Materialism', p. 231.

58 Ibid.

59 Ibid.

60 Ibid.

61 See S. Coldham, 'Land Reform and Customary Rights in Uganda', *Journal of African Law*, 44 (2000), pp. 65–77.

62 Government of Uganda, *Report of the Land Act Implementation Study* (Kampala: Ministry of Lands, 1999).

63 For an account see McAuslan, *Bringing the Law Back In*, in particular Chapters 12 ('As Good as It Gets: Politics and Markets in the Making of Uganda's Land Act, 1998') and 13 ('Men Behaving Badly: A Narrative of Land Reform').

64 See A. Manji, 'Commodifying Land, Fetishising Law: Women's Struggles to Claim Land Rights in Uganda', *Australian Feminist Law Journal*, 19 (2003), pp. 81–92.

65 Patrick McAuslan, personal communication.

66 McAuslan, *Bringing the Law Back In*, pp. 272–3.

67 Cutler, 'Historical Materialism'.

4 Making law: inside the 'law laboratory'

A striking feature of the last two decades, which has received surprisingly little attention from academic commentators and policy-makers, has been the part played by lawyers in the contemporary land reform process. In this chapter, I offer a means by which to model the role of lawyers in land reform, arguing that it is important to be alert to the agency of lawyers, to the ways in which they have acted on society,[1] as well as to the political and economic context in which they have come to play an important role. For this purpose, I find the work of Bruno Latour in the sociology of science to be particularly helpful. Little is known about the everyday work of lawyers, and in particular of the efforts of technical legal consultants, in land reform. A detailed anthropological study of their role awaits an author. What is offered here for the first time is a proposed model by which it might be possible to understand their important and hitherto overlooked contribution. Based not on first-hand observation but on analyses of the accounts of those involved in the field of technical legal consultancy, this chapter subjects the work of lawyers in land reform projects to sociological analysis for the first time.

Debates about legal methodology have also been a prominent feature of African land reform to date and I wish to demonstrate in this chapter that decisions about how to use the law, far from being a technical intra-legal issue, are deeply connected with political and economic choices. I argue that it is significant that deliberations about legal methodology have characterized the contemporary 'law laboratory' and that the persistence today of these debates echoes those of the early law and development movement. This suggests that there may be a striking similarity between the concerns of the original and the recently revived law and development movements.

The role of lawyers

In his writing on the mystery of capital, Hernando de Soto has observed:

> [a]lthough entrepreneurs and ordinary people are the builders of capital and of capitalism, it is the lawyers who fix property concepts in tangible representative form and define those concepts in statutes. The security of ownership, the accountability of owners and the enforceability of transactions must ultimately be concretised in procedures and rules drafted by lawyers. It is the legal profession that perfects all the artefacts of formal property.[2]

In this passage, the celebrated economist is drawing attention to an important element of the global network of land reform: the role of lawyers. De Soto recognizes their responsibility for 'perfect[ing] all the artefacts of formal property', for ensuring security of ownership and the enforceability of contracts, and for setting out the detailed rules and procedures relating to dealings in land. The work of lawyers can be said to underpin both the current transition to individualized land tenure and the future functioning of land markets. In the discussion that follows, I explore the role of the technical legal consultants – Patrick McAuslan, whose work is discussed in detail below, has described them as 'legal policy-makers'[3] – who, it will be seen, have played a central role in the transformation of land relations currently underway.

As I have already noted, one of the most important primary sources of information and insight for those interested in the place of technical legal consultants in the global politics of land reform is the writing of Patrick McAuslan, a law professor at the University of London and a leading figure in the field. As well as his role as a consultant, McAuslan has written extensive academic

79

reflections on his work, providing invaluable perspectives on a field that would otherwise remain rather technical, bureaucratic and inaccessible. He has done so deliberately, arguing that 'trying to give some wider publicity to one's work as a consultant is part of the duties of a consultant ... [t]oo often, consultants' reports are deemed to be confidential or where they are available for circulation, do not in practice receive wide publicity and so do not circulate outside a very restricted circle'.[4]

In his academic work, McAuslan has offered vivid accounts of the process of land law reform, describing the world of international donors, law-makers, consultants, ministry officials and bureaucrats, thereby furnishing us with glimpses of the everyday workings of the network of land reform. For this reason, and due to his prominence as a technical legal consultant, McAuslan's writing is an important source for those seeking to understand the discrete section of the network of land reform that I describe as the 'law laboratory'. However, it is important to stress that the analysis provided here is concerned not with any individual technical legal consultant but with the *role* itself, seeking to investigate and explain its centrality to land reform at this time.

In Chapter 3, I raised briefly the question of why law has come to prominence as a solution to the perceived problems associated with land, asking: why is it that in recent years land reform has come in practice to mean land *law* reform?[5] I wish to explore this question in greater depth in what follows. Drawing on Latour's work on the construction of the scientific laboratory and its place in the social milieu and on his elaboration of the 'moves' necessary to establish the interests of outsiders in the laboratory's project, I attempt to trace the role of lawyers in promoting law as a way to address land problems, tackle poverty and promote economic growth. My aim is to explore the contribution of technical legal consultants, a contribution which has gone largely unremarked until now and has therefore remained underanalysed. More broadly, the analysis presented here is concerned with how the efforts of technical legal consultants might be said to signal a revival of a network of law in development scholarship and practice.

It is evident from de Soto's comment cited above that in his view law is central to contemporary land reform, given the emphasis of the latter on formalization and individual tenure, and on making land available as collateral. McAuslan has pointed out that an additional explanation for the law's prominence is to be found in the embrace by donors of the language of good governance. Thus:

> the twin emphasis of donors, led by the World Bank, on 'good governance' and the market economy as the keys to social and economic regeneration in Africa are increasingly seen as necessitating a greater reliance on legal forms and a legal culture similar to those operating in Western, market oriented economies; conscious moves to adapt legal and judicial systems to that end are thus increasingly part of aid programmes.[6]

In consequence, as the discussion in Chapter 2 shows, land reform in the contemporary era has come to be equated with – and is all too often treated as reducible to – tenure reform, in which the law necessarily plays a central part.

I am to some extent persuaded by McAuslan's assertion that we can discover an explanation for donors' increased resort to law in the fact that they emphasize both the market economy and the achievement of good governance as the keys to bringing about Africa's development, and that this leads them to attach great significance to the legal forms and culture which are taken to characterize Western societies and economies. This is the analysis of a scholar occupying a position both within the British legal academy and within the world of legal consultancy who has gained vital insights into the practical and theoretical development of the land reform field. However, what remains obscured by this analysis, with its emphasis on the motivations of those who *seek* legal solutions to development problems, is the story of those who *promote* legal solutions. If law has come to be seen as central to the resolution of Africa's land problems, this is in no small part due to the interventions and activities of lawyers, and more specifically legal consultants, themselves. This is an issue that has tended to be overlooked in discussions of land reform to date with the result that neither scholars of land reform nor those concerned with the field of law and development have adequately explained the curious translation of the issue of land reform into one of law reform. The important role of agency in the land reform project has received little attention with the consequence that the strenuous efforts of key individuals in the land reform process to ensure that legal solutions are sought for the problems of land relations have gone unnoticed, as if there was an inevitability about the law's intervention in the field. In contrast to this approach, I would argue that it is precisely through the entrepreneurial activities of legal professionals that the law has come to have a central place in land reform.

'The law laboratory' in the network of land reform

In this section, I formulate a theory of the role of agency in the increasingly important world of legal consultancy and in this way begin to analyse the relationship between law and politics that characterizes contemporary land reform. I argue that, in order to do this, it is important to understand technical legal consultants as 'acting on society' and to ask how and why they have come to be 'credible' spokespeople for land law reform.[7] If in Chapter 3 the focus was on those who seek legal solutions to land issues – the World Bank and bilateral donors who view the formalization of land relations as an important aspect of economic development – in this chapter I turn my attention to the work of those who promote such legal solutions.

There is a sense in much writing on contemporary land reform that there is an inexorable progress entailed in using law as a way to alter land relations. The emphasis is on how international financial institutions, bilateral donors and national governments have, seemingly of their own accord, looked to the legal sphere for solutions to land problems. These depictions obscure the reality that, in the past decade or more, legal responses to problems of land relations have been energetically promoted. As well as those who turn to the legal sphere for solutions to land problems, therefore, we should pay attention to the role played by those who advocate them. The emphasis on the rule of law as a development strategy, discussed in Chapter 1, should not distract us from the fact that tenure reform is but one method for confronting land problems and for altering the ways in which land is dealt with. That tenure reform rather than redistribution has come to characterize land reform in the present day is the result of a series of political and economic choices, among them the choice to prioritize a functioning market economy over the provision of secure livelihoods and to promote the idea of land as a form collateral rather than as a means to tackle landlessness and poverty.

In his account of the development and functioning of networks, Latour showed how it was important to pay attention to 'the construction of the lab and its position in the social milieu'.[8] For Latour, it was by heeding what went on inside the laboratory that it was possible to explain the 'interest of outsiders' in its work for, as Latour shows in the case of Pasteur, there was a great deal of work entailed in 'enrolling and enlisting them'.[9] The scientific laboratory thus became the site of Latour's investigations. Similarly, I am interested in this chapter in what might be described as the 'law laboratory' of the technical legal consultant. My aim is to cast light on what might be occurring inside such law laboratories and to explore the work that takes place inside them, work about which we know little.

Latour elucidates three 'moves' necessary to enlisting the interest of outsiders in the work of the laboratory.[10] 'Move one' entails 'capturing others' interests'.[11] Before setting out how

Latour's analysis might cast light on the work of technical legal consultants involved in today's land reform projects, it is useful to explore the concrete examples he used to illustrate his analysis. In order to demonstrate how the capturing of interests occurred in the context of Pasteur's science, Latour demonstrated that before Pasteur's intervention, diseases were local events about which there existed only 'careful, variable, prudent and uncertain knowledge'.[12] The task facing Pasteur was, therefore, 'to learn from the field, translating each item of veterinary science into [his] own terms'.[13] Pasteur, working in a makeshift lab on the farm itself, learning from the field and functioning in the centre of a world previously 'untouched by laboratory science',[14] achieved this preliminary step by successfully translating issues of veterinary science into his own terms.

Latour identifies the second step necessary to establishing Pasteur's science as an 'obligatory point of passage' as 'moving the lever point from a weak to a strong position'.[15] Once again offering an illustration of this step, Latour describes how this is done by making the hitherto invisible micro-organism visible inside the laboratory. As he puts it: 'having designated the micro-organism as the living and pertinent cause, he can now reformulate farmers' interests in a new way: if you wish to solve *your* problem you have to pass through *my* lab first'.[16]

The next step necessary in Pasteur's project to enlist the interest of others in his science is described by Latour as one of 'moving the world with the lever'.[17] The importance of this move lies in the fact that something more than laboratory studies must take place if the interests of different groups which have been enrolled are not to fade and disperse. Interestingly, Latour characterizes the translation of interests by Pasteur (essentially 'solve your problems through Pasteur's laboratory')[18] as part of a contract, 'the counterpart of which is now expected from Pasteur'.[19] What is entailed in performing this part of the contract? The answer is 'a return to the farm to show results', a return which

Latour characterizes as a 'staging' in the sense of a performance.[20] Before this move is made, the contract was simply 'solve your problems through my microbiology'.[21] After the staging of the return to the farm, the translation is, 'if you want to save your animals from anthrax, order a vaccine flask from Pasteur's lab'.[22] Latour calls this 'the displacement of laboratories'.[23]

How might we employ these detailed insights into the sociology of science to model the work of today's land-related legal consultants? How, in other words, might we identify the moves necessary to establish land law reform as 'an obligatory point of passage'?[24] Drawing on Latour's explanatory framework, we can suggest that there are a number of moves that must be executed by those who advocate legal solutions to land problems. Move one consists in capturing the interests of others, in 'convincing others of what their interests are and what they ought to want and to be'.[25] In the field of land reform, technical legal consultants who have played a key role in advocating the resolution of land problems through the use of law have done so by successfully intervening to assist in the difficult task of addressing contradictory demands in relation to land. Rural inhabitants faced with long-running problems of land grabbing, as well as chaotic systems of land administration, called on the government to address these grievances. In their turn, international financial institutions began to perceive land reform as intricately connected to questions of good governance and the efficient operation of a market economy (and, as the experience of the last two decades of land reform amply demonstrate, the demands of the Bretton Woods institutions and foreign investors are wont to take precedence over the needs of the rural poor). These two developments do not in themselves explain how it came to be that legal solutions played a prominent role in land reform. It is at this point that the role of the lawyer becomes important. As experts, the skill of land-related technical legal consultants lies in 'fostering interest groups and persuading their members that their interests were

Making law

inseparable from his own'.[26] As such, the boundaries between what international financial institutions, bilateral donors and African governments want and what technical legal consultants 'make them want' are blurred. It is, however, clear that the new land laws that have emerged in Africa in the last two decades are the consequence of the fact that international financial institutions, bilateral donors and African governments 'accepted to pass through [his] hands in order to solve their problems'.[27]

The second move necessary in establishing what might be described as the 'law laboratory' as 'an obligatory point of passage' would involve those advocating legal solutions in identifying the pertinent cause of the problem faced by African societies. This is done, according to Latour's model, by making visible in the laboratory that which has hitherto been invisible. Extended to land reform, it might be said that the task facing the lawyer is to make apparent that which has until now been overlooked. The diagnosis is therefore offered: if you have lacked development, it is because dead capital is tied up in your land. As we saw in Chapter 1, such an analysis has widespread currency at the present time. Having thus designated non-formalized land tenure as the cause of underdevelopment, technical legal consultants propagate the message (to paraphrase Latour) that if the third world wants to solve its problems, it must pass through the law laboratory.

The third necessary move requires the technical legal consultant to guard against the interests he has captured from fading and dispersing. He must emerge from his law laboratory and return to 'the farm' to show his results. The staging of results 'on the farm' is the crucial step which transforms the message from 'if you want to solve your development problems solve them through my land law', to 'if you want to save your countries from underdevelopment, if you want to alleviate poverty, order a law from my laboratory'.

For Latour, the effect of networks is to collapse space. Latour points out that '[t]he negotiation of the equivalence of non-equivalent situations is always what characterises the spread of a science'.[28] The process of negotiating equivalence has been a characteristic of contemporary work in African land law. It might be said to have entailed the collapsing of geographical space in that disparate African countries find themselves with similar land laws framed to facilitate the privatization of land. It is, however, important to recognize the political and economic context in which equivalence is negotiated. Latour provides a striking metaphor to explain the structural context for the spread of science: 'Scientific facts are like trains. They do not work off their rails. You can extend the rail and connect them but you cannot drive a locomotive through a field.'[29] For the purposes of understanding contemporary African land reform, the rails that carry the locomotive of the law are constructed, extended and maintained by multilateral and bilateral aid donors such as the World Bank and the British Department for International Development (DfID) which, as I have shown in Chapter 3, have played a central role in funding land law reform in Africa since the early 1990s.

The work of technical legal advisers can be interpreted as attempts to translate the interests of a number of important actors into the language of African law reform. This is apparent from the following passage in which McAuslan sets out an ambitious agenda for lawyers involved in land law reform:

Lawyers, and particularly academic lawyers ... face ... the challenge of scholarship; to rise above the merely descriptive and analytical approach to writing about land law and adopt a more policy-oriented and innovative approach which offers new models and creative ideas as solutions to practical problems of land management; and, if the opportunity presents itself, to become involved in the challenging business of turning these ideas and models into legislative drafts – a scholarly endeavour, for which creative and not just critical scholarship is needed.[30]

It can be predicted that technical legal consultants will also be required to play a central role in sustaining the network of land law reform into the future. This will no doubt be necessitated by the sheer scale of the new administrative machineries often initiated by new land legislation. In Uganda, for instance, the new land administration required the creation of forty-five entirely new district Land Boards and 9,000 parish-level Land Committees. At the national level, a Land Committee is responsible for holding and managing government land.[31] At the district level, Land Boards[32] will have a variety of powers and will be responsible, inter alia, for confirming, rejecting or varying the recommendations of Land Committees in relation to certificates of customary ownership[33] and for playing a role in the conversion of customary tenure to freehold tenure.[34] The District Council also contains a District Land Office which is constituted by a physical planner, a land officer, a valuer, a surveyor and a registrar of titles.[35] A Land Committee which functions at the parish level is appointed by the District Council.[36] These committees are responsible for the initial consideration of certificates of customary ownership, applications for grants of land in freehold and applications to convert customary tenure to freehold tenure. Finally, each district has a Land Tribunal with jurisdiction over land disputes.

Given the extent of the changes initiated by Uganda's 1998 Land Act, Simon Coldham, a lawyer who has written on African land issues, has identified the recruitment, training and support of personnel as a key issue for the future. He has argued:

> It will be essential to train the cadres who will be responsible for implementing the Act. In addition to increasing significantly the number of surveyors, planners and registrars, it will be essential to train the members of all the new administrative bodies ... destined to play a central role in the process ... While an extensive recruitment and training exercise will add substantially to the cost, the land reform programme is already controversial

and, if it is carried out in a way that is insensitive or inept, it will leave behind a legacy of disputes and bitterness.[37]

The ongoing relevance and future success of the network is guaranteed by future needs for the implementation and training of the personnel necessary to run the vast new machineries of land administration.

The politics of legal methodology

The importance of a legal system which promotes certainty in a functioning market economy has been noted as much by the World Bank and Hernando de Soto as by legal consultants such as McAuslan, the latter arguing that this is the main reason why law must be brought 'back in'.[38] Much in evidence here is faith that the law will achieve equity, efficiency and certainty in land relations. For McAuslan, these values are explicitly described as 'essential national interests' that should be enshrined in any national land policy.[39] A further, related reason why law is perceived to have an important contribution to make to the terrain of land reform is that it will come to replace administrative discretion, which is viewed as having caused many difficulties in land relations. For McAuslan, the experience of South Africa serves as evidence of the problems of discretionary powers:

> law was used to abolish law. Land reform in South Africa then must include land *law* reform because it seeks to change the nature of the legal regime and legal culture that applies to African-held land. It is to replace, at best, licences or permits held at the mercy of administrators or chiefs, with *rights* guaranteed by law.[40]

In Tanzania the same reasoning pertains: 'land reform is preeminently land *law* reform: the substitution of a law to facilitate the *right* of citizens to access and hold land, for a law which had facilitated the state's *administrative control* over the citizens' access to land'.[41]

89

How these twin objectives – the promotion of the legal certainty that is conducive to a market economy and the replacement of administrative discretion with specific legal rights – might be achieved has been a major preoccupation of those charged with reviewing Africa's land laws and new legislation. As a result, one of the most important tasks facing technical legal consultants has been to ascertain the appropriate style of legal drafting to be used. This might be described as an issue of legal methodology and broadly speaking, centres round the question of how much law to use. The importance of legal methodology lies in the fact that the style of legal drafting that is chosen will determine how much power is allocated to bureaucrats through land laws. Tanzania's efforts at land reform – beginning in 1991 and culminating (at least formally) in the passing of the Land Act 1998 and the Village Land Act 1998 – provided an excellent example of contestation over issues of legal methodology.

There was considerable disagreement over this issue in Tanzania when McAuslan first wrote the National Land Policy document and then drafted two new land bills. The Tanzanian experience of land reform was marked by fierce disagreements between McAuslan, as the legal consultant in charge of producing two new land bills, and Shivji, as head of the sidelined Presidential Commission of Inquiry into Land Matters, about the purpose and direction of such reform, the content of the proposed legislation and the legal methodology to be adopted. Perhaps by virtue of being members of the academy, Shivji and McAuslan spoke and wrote about their views of land reform – and their differences with each other – in great detail, enabling those studying the politics of land to follow closely the course of the debate.[42] As regards legal methodology, the main disagreement between McAuslan and Shivji focused on what might be described as the 'more law/less law' divide. In Shivji's view, the proposed land bills were unworkable because they set out in intricate detail the powers and responsibilities of bureaucrats in the land administration machinery and sought to exert detailed control over their actions. Shivji was critical of this approach, arguing that it trampled on traditional community methods of controlling the exercise of discretion by public officials.[43] McAuslan, on the other hand, adhered to the view that it was important for the new land law to set out in as much detail as possible the duties of those charged with the administration of land. He recommended and sought to achieve 'a detailed and inevitably lengthy new land code in which legal rules and checks and balances replace reliance on administrative and political action based on goodwill and common sense – which, according to the evidence, are in short supply where land relations are concerned'.[44]

These different approaches to the methodology of land law cannot be understood apart from the wider disputes about the purpose and direction of land reform that characterized the Tanzanian experience. As will be recalled from Chapter 2, the Report of the Shivji Commission made a number of key recommendations which were, inter alia, that radical title to land be divested from the government and vested in the village assemblies and an extra-executive body to be called the National Commission of Lands, and also that the powerful Ministry of Lands be abolished.[45] The approach taken by McAuslan was diametrically opposed to that of the Shivji Commission. McAuslan's bills had as their objective the creation of a suitable environment for investment in land by large-scale buyers and the setting up of an efficient system for a market in land.

The extent of the difference in approach taken by Shivji and McAuslan in key policy documents had a profound effect on their perception of the appropriate legal methodology to be adopted in Tanzania. For McAuslan: 'Law was, and to some extent still is, perceived in Tanzania as an impediment to change; therefore, where the law has to be used, the style of drafting has tended to be one of conferring powers on officials, with few safeguards or external controls.'[46] In contrast, Shivji argued that there did in fact exist a number of mechanisms for community control of public officials charged with the allocation of land and other tasks such as dispute resolution. In fact, these opposing approaches are explained not so much by historical preferences but by contemporary reality. McAuslan's land bills sought to create a vast new machinery of land administration and this alone necessitated the detailed legal provisions he favoured. It had little to do with history as McAuslan suggests: 'the clear message of the Presidential Commission was that the new law should be similar to that which it will replace in terms of drafting style, with a few broad strokes of the legal pen giving vast powers to legally unqualified people and relying on their innate common-sense and sense of justice to get things done'.[47]

Under the scheme recommended by the Shivji Commission, a far smaller land bureaucracy would have come into being and a less precise conferral of exact powers might have been workable. In the law laboratory, then, the style of legal methodology that is adopted will be influenced in part by the style of land administration that is favoured. I return to this issue in Chapter 6 where I discuss some of the problems that are likely to arise in relation to the administration of land in the future and deal specifically with the difficulties of implementation to which this can be expected to give rise.

It is from the perspective of public law that McAuslan approached the task of developing land policy and drafting legislation. Because both private and public law operate to define property rights and, furthermore, when land is allocated by the state, this requires the private citizen to deal with public officials, 'land law ceases to be a matter of private law, but becomes part of public law; it is in fact, administrative law'.[48] McAuslan's ideas of the role that law should play in regulating land relations come predominantly from public law. Notions such as public accountability or the exercise of discretion that play a prominent role in McAuslan's view of what land law should achieve, can only be understood as deriving from McAuslan's wider work as a public lawyer.[49] Indeed, McAuslan refers to 'using law as an administrative tool'.[50] His caution about public officials and bureaucrats derives from his public law background, as evidenced by his assertion that 'officials armed with powers and subject to few or no restraints, cannot be relied upon to behave reasonably'.[51]

For McAuslan, the South African approach to legislative drafting that favours detailed codes of law is the most likely to be workable:

> Administrative law or administrative justice requires that official power be bounded by legal rules, be exercised in accordance with certain principles of fairness, allows for hearings and appeals, and be subject to review. How else can this be done except through statutory provisions which go beyond merely granting powers to officials, to setting out the matter and form of their exercise and control?[52]

In his view, a dual test thus had to be applied to new Tanzanian legislation: 'did it create a new substantive land law, appropriate to the conditions of Tanzania; and, did it provide a suitable legal framework for the exercise of powers by officials?'[53]

According to McAuslan, the existence of the market requires more rather than less law: 'once the land law recognises and protects private rights, and facilitates dealings with those private rights in the market place the law has to be much more specific, detailed and clear'.[54] The law must provide for the market's need for certainty. This recalls the discussion in Chapter 1 in which it was argued that the revival of interest in using the law to bring about development may be characterized as 'new wave' law in development in the age of neo-liberalism. This is in marked contrast to the law in development of the late 1960s to the mid-1970s, which was concerned primarily with the promotion of state-centred economic development.

McAuslan's discussion of the market's need for detailed and

specific law is suggestive. However, it does not make fully explicit the nature of the market which it is being sought to promote, that is, one which is dominated by foreign investors. A similar task faced another, earlier legal scholar and technical legal consultant. When Professor L. C. B. Gower of University College London was charged with drafting a new company law for the newly independent Ghana, he too grappled with similar issues of legal methodology. For Gower, the question was whether and by which means to give the registrar of companies enhanced powers. Describing the drafting dilemma with which he was thus confronted, Gower wrote: 'It would, no doubt, have been possible to produce something shorter by adopting a different drafting technique ... I am certainly not averse from giving the Registrar enhanced powers ... [but] if one goes too far in the way of substituting administrative discretion and regulation for fixed statutory rules one destroys certainty.'[55] Gower made explicit reference to the difficulties he thought might be caused by awarding wide discretionary powers to the registrar of companies, going so far as to express his fear that the negative impact of allowing wide discretionary powers in legislation might be felt even if such discretion were in reality to be properly exercised. He put it as follows:

> The man-on-the-spot knows that discretions are exercised fairly and reasonably; the men-at-home read the regulation, see the width of the discretions, and fear and expect the worst. And, of course, it is the fearful men-at-home who control the purse-strings and decide what capital is invested in Ghana. The lesson, once again, is that legislation and regulations affecting the foreign investor should be drafted in such a way as to encourage him to hope and expect the best rather than to fear the worst. It is no answer to say that when he (and his capital) arrives they will find that his fears are unfounded; he will never arrive to find out.[56]

Gower was an early participant in technical legal work funded at the time by the Britain–Ghana technical assistance programme. He was thus a key figure in early law and development.[57] I have suggested that the recent work of legal consultants in the field of land reform signals a reincarnation of the field of law and development. It is therefore interesting to note that many of the concerns and preoccupations of the revived field of law and development remain the same: the role of law in the encouragement of foreign investors, the scope of administrative discretion, the importance of investors' perceptions of law even where discretion is in fact properly exercised and the appropriate legal drafting style to adopt. The debates over legal methodology discussed above – both in the immediate post-independence period and more recently – should serve to remind us that such struggles are not intra-legal technical battles but are deeply imbricated in political and economic choices.

Conclusion

Until now, accounts of land reform in the present era have neglected the fact that the translation of issues of land reform into technical, legal questions was not inevitable. If law has played a central role in African land reform, I have argued that it must be recognized that this is in part as a consequence of the activities of those in the legal field who have sought to enlist and enrol the interests of outsiders. I have argued that the early law in development movement came into being as a result of the efforts of legal scholars who sought to translate the interests of newly independent states into issues of law. After having fallen into disuse for some time, as such interests faded and dispersed, the law and development movement is now being revived by the efforts of legal consultants who seek to 'bring the law back in'.[58] I have also shown in this chapter that the work of lawyers on the new laws aimed at liberalizing land relations has been centrally concerned with issues of legal methodology, such as the most effective means by which to control the exercise of discretion and encourage foreign investment. Far from being an exercise in the technicalities of how best to draft new laws, I have sought to show here that choices as to legal methodology are deeply political.

Notes

1 B. Latour, 'Give Me a Laboratory and I Will Raise the World', in K. D. Knorr-Cetina and M. Mulkay (eds), *Science Observed: Perspectives in the Social Study of Science* (London: Sage, 1983), p. 157.

2 H. de Soto, *The Mystery of Capital: Why Capitalism Triumphs in the West and Fails Everywhere Else* (London: Black Swan, 2000), pp. 209–10.

3 P. McAuslan, *Bringing the Law Back In: Essays in Land, Law and Development* (Aldershot: Ashgate, 2003).

4 Ibid., p. viii.

5 As I note in Chapter 3, this question is posed by Patrick McAuslan in ibid.

6 Ibid., p. 245.

7 Latour, 'Give Me a Laboratory', p. 157.

8 Ibid., p. 142.

9 Ibid., p. 143.

10 Ibid., p. 145.

11 Ibid., p. 144.

12 Ibid.

13 Ibid.

14 Ibid.

15 Ibid., p. 146.

16 Ibid. (italics in the original).

17 Ibid., p. 150.

18 Ibid.

19 Ibid.

20 Ibid., p. 152.

21 Ibid.

22 Ibid.

23 Ibid.

24 Ibid., p. 144.

25 Ibid.

26 Ibid., p. 150.

27 Ibid.

28 Ibid., p. 155.

29 Ibid.

30 McAuslan, *Bringing the Law Back In*, p. 272.

31 S 47 and S 50, Uganda Land Act 1998.

32 S 57, Uganda Land Act 1998.

33 S 8, Uganda Land Act 1998.

34 S 10–14, Uganda Land Act 1998.

35 S 60 (6), Uganda Land Act 1998.

36 S 65 (1), Uganda Land Act 1998.

37 S. Coldham, 'Land Reform and Customary Rights in Uganda', *Journal of African Law*, 44 (2000), pp. 65–77.

38 McAuslan, *Bringing the Law Back In*, p. 256.

39 Ibid., pp. 8–15.

40 Ibid., p. 248 (author's italics).

41 Ibid., p. 249.

42 For a detailed study of this period, see G. Sundet, *The Politics of Land in Tanzania*, Unpublished D. Phil. thesis, University of Oxford, 1997.

43 I. G. Shivji and W. Kapinga, 'Implications of the Draft Bill for the Land Act', *Change*, 5 (1997), p. 62.

44 McAuslan, *Bringing the Law Back In*, p. 254.

45 The government did not look with pleasure on recommendations which would abolish its monopoly of the radical title to land and thereby substantially alter the structure of the state. The Commission's report was designed not to operationalize a land market, but on the contrary to control the alienation of land and guarantee security of tenure for peasant producers. In Shivji's assessment, in appointing the Commission of Inquiry into Land Matters, 'what was anticipated was a report that would rationalise and legitimate the impending liberalisation of land in line with the policy diktat of the international financial institutions'. See I. G. Shivji, 'Contradictory Perspectives on Rights and Justice in the Context of Land Tenure Reform in Tanzania', Paper presented to a meeting of the Academic Staff Council, University of Dar es Salaam, 1997.

46 McAuslan, *Bringing the Law Back In*, p. 252.

47 Ibid., p. 253.

48 Ibid., p. 255.

49 See M. Loughlin, *Public Law and Political Theory* (Oxford: Clarendon Press, 1992).

50 McAuslan, *Bringing the Law Back In*, p. 255.

51 Ibid.

52 Ibid., p. 256.

53 Ibid.

54 Ibid.

55 L. C. B. Gower, *Final Report of the Commission of Enquiry into the Working and Administration of the Present Company Law of Ghana* (Accra: Government of Ghana, 1961), pp. 5–6.

56 Ibid., p. 11.

57 J. Harrington and A. Manji, 'The Emergence of African Law as an Academic Discipline in Britain', *African Affairs*, 102 (2003), pp. 109–34.

58 McAuslan, *Bringing the Law Back In*.

5 Contesting law? 'Gender progressive' groups and rural movements

In this chapter I maintain a focus on the revival of interest in using law to bring about development. Exploring law's role in contemporary land reform, I seek to investigate why it might be that the emphasis on law in contemporary land reform in Africa has remained largely uncontested. To do this, I turn to a further section of the network of African land reform and explore the part played by 'gender progressive' groups, such as women's advocacy groups and non-governmental organizations (NGOs) in recent years. I employ the term 'gender progressive' groups coined by Agarwal in her extensive study of women's land rights in South Asia to refer to organizations concerned with reducing or eliminating the social, economic and political inequalities facing women in relation to men.[1] I argue that such gender progressive groups have rarely challenged the emphasis placed by international financial institutions, donors, governments and technical legal consultants on law as the solution to the problems of land relations. Indeed, I argue that their engagement in the land reform process has affirmed rather than questioned the use of law to bring about development. In so doing, it has neglected to confront the difficult distributional choices entailed in any discussion of land relations. Rather, gender progressive groups have themselves embraced the language of good governance and the rule of law being promoted by international financial institutions such as the World Bank and by bilateral aid donors such as Britain. If the last decade or so has witnessed a revival of law and development, gender progressive civil society groups have been central to this process. As I show, they have tended to adopt a technical, instrumentalist approach to law that has in fact limited their scope for action. Rather than challenging its methods, gender progressive groups have played an important role in sustaining a network of land law reform. To illustrate this argument, I present two case studies, the first from Tanzania and the second focusing on Uganda, exploring the work of gender progressive groups on land issues and the extent and nature of their engagement in the land reform process in these two countries.

In the second part of this chapter, I discuss the emergence of rural movements and seek to show how the methods they have employed can be distinguished from those of gender progressive groups. Formed in response to the unequal distribution of land, and aiming to challenge this state of affairs, rural movements have shown themselves to be sceptical of the state and of state law. They have adopted oppositional strategies such as land invasions that allow scope for state law to recognize their claims but that are not founded primarily on appealing to the state to provide solutions to their problems. Rather, rural movements have taken the initiative on unequal distribution of land, claiming tenure rights over it and allocating it to beneficiaries. In some cases, these tenurial arrangements meet with subsequent confirmation by the law but it is clear that this is not the main aim of rural movements when they organize and carry out land invasions. I argue that in marked contrast to gender progressive groups, rural movements have functioned outside the contemporary network of land law reform.

Case studies: gender progressive groups in East Africa

The analysis contained in this section focuses on the larger registered women's associations in both Tanzania and Uganda. There are two reasons for this. First, due to their size and expressed aims, larger associations were vocal on a number of key land issues and were therefore best placed to lobby on such matters. Second, while numerous informal organizations do exist in both Tanzania and Uganda, their ability to make themselves heard is limited by their disparate and informal nature.

Gender and tenure reform in Tanzania The formation of non-governmental organizations with the purpose of tackling gender issues in Tanzania dates from the mid-1980s. At their forefront was the Tanzania Gender Networking Programme (TGNP) which was formed in 1992 to coordinate women's associations in preparation for the East African Women's Conference in Kampala the following year. It subsequently came to act as an umbrella organization for gender related groups and had as one of its main declared objectives the promotion of pressure groups to lobby for policy changes at national and local levels.[2] TGNP, together with a professional body, the Tanzania Women Lawyers' Association, became involved in discussions on the land question only after the new land bill and village land bill were made public in 1997. In that year, international women's day was dedicated specifically to women's land rights under the slogan *Ardhi ni Haki ya Wanawake* (Land is Women's Right). After a conspicuous absence, this entry on to the scene was sudden. Women's groups had not sought to influence the work of the presidential inquiry into land matters which travelled all over the country hearing the views of rural dwellers. In consequence, the Commission's extensive report dedicated only four pages to discussing the issue of women's access to and rights over land. Women's groups were also conspicuously absent from discussions on the national land policy, responsibility for which was vested in the Ministry of Lands in November 1995.

Women's groups in Tanzania thus came relatively late to participate in the land tenure reform debate. Their involvement became discernible only after the draft land laws had been drawn up. At that stage, they intervened by formulating responses to the proposed laws and by issuing detailed commentaries on them.[3] Given the political and economic importance of land and property rights to women, and the recognition of this fact in a range of international law instruments, one might have expected women's groups to play a key role from the inception of the land reform debate. This was not the case: in reality, the earliest stages of the land debate were characterized by a lack of engagement by women's groups which proved to be remarkably ineffective in advocacy on land matters.

One explanation for the neglect of the land issue by the Tanzanian women's movement may be sought in its traditional emphasis on the issue of employment. Drawing on a substantial body of feminist work in this area, advocates of gender equality had focused on female employment rather than land ownership or control as a significant factor affecting women's position in society.[4] This was an approach that has been widely adopted by feminist groups, not only in Africa but also in South Asia.[5] It was influenced and reinforced by the attitude of government departments and their bias in policy towards employment issues. At the height of the land reform debate in Tanzania, TGNP's key policy document, a 'Gender Profile of Tanzania', contained a detailed situational analysis of women in Tanzania and, in its review of strategies for change, indicated a preoccupation with female employment in the formal and informal sectors of the economy. The issue of women's access to or independent rights in land did not feature on the policy agenda of TGNP.[6]

The second reason why gender progressive groups proved weak during the land tenure reform debate was their overly legalistic and simplistic approach to the issue. The Tanzanian land debate was remarkable for its lack of detailed theorization of how the proposed changes would affect women. There was no attempt to set out an independent policy position regarding women's relations to land. The contribution of women's groups was, late in the process, to debate the provisions of the draft legislation once this was made public and at a time when the direction of land reform had arguably already been determined. This technocratic approach was an important factor in the failure of the women's movement in Tanzania to address the crucial issues facing women in relation to land. The preoccupation with the details of legal formulations in the draft land bills limited the ability of women's groups to formulate their basic demands. They assumed that problematic aspects of the bills could be remedied simply by suggesting minor textual amendments. Their preference for quick-fix solutions to aspects of the draft legislation meant that they took an over-simplistic view of the problems at hand which it was assumed would be adequately addressed by legalistic solutions.

Gender aspects of the land question in Tanzania were debated in closed shops by a limited number of individuals. At a workshop held in Dar es Salaam in 1997, for example, the draft land bill was reviewed in order to recommend minor amendments and the focus of the meeting was on how Parliament might be effectively lobbied to achieve the desired amendments.[7] The proceedings of the workshop reveal that detailed attention was paid to provision after provision of the draft legislation with little regard to the wider question of the demands of rural women and how they might be met, for example through a programme of land redistribution.[8] Aspects of the draft bill discussed during the consultative workshop included the weakness of some interpretation clauses, ambiguities in the construction of legal terms, and the powers vested in the Commissioner for Land by the bill.[9] Tampering with aspects of the bill in this way was evidence of the marginality of gender progressive voices in the process. The technicist approach that was adopted deflected women's groups from addressing the broader political pressure for land reform as well as more fundamental shortcomings of the legislation.

The failure to engage with policy debates on land issues also revealed an inherent weakness in the women's movement in Tanzania. This was their urban bias. This explained why women's groups were slow to respond to the beginning of the national land reform process. One illustration of urban bias was the Media

Watch project of the TGNP, the purpose of which was to protest sexist language and writing in the media. Without wishing to detract from the importance of battles against sexism, it is clear that the priority attached to the project was unwarranted. There were clearly a number of more pressing issues facing Tanzanian women at that time, as there are today, and it might have been expected that women's groups would have been alert to these. Land was one issue among them.

As well as suggesting the urban bias of women's groups, this example also revealed the extent to which the agenda of such groups has been donor-driven. The issues being tackled are most often a reflection not of local needs, conditions and priorities but of the issues receiving attention in Western countries. The direct transplantation of Western feminist concerns to Tanzania bears the advantage that the activities of women's groups are easily 'read' by donors on whom they are reliant for aid. Many gender-related NGOs formed in Tanzania in response to the promulgation of international law instruments such as Convention for the Elimination of Discrimination Against Women (CEDAW).[10] These NGOs act essentially as foreign-funded watchdogs on behalf of international agencies, such as the United Nations, for example by providing alternative country reports on the progress being made by governments in implementing and adopting the principles of CEDAW by legislative and other means.[11] They need to ensure that their work is recognizable to and capable of validation by an external constituency. A consequence of this international law imperialism in Tanzania was that the more complex issues affecting the global south, issues of economic deprivation and unequal access to productive resources by women, were allowed to fall by the wayside. The class composition of the women's movement also affected the ability of urban, middle-class women to address the concerns of rural constituents. Land is a scarce and valuable resource and to members of a post-colonial bourgeoisie with the ability to invest in land, either individually or collectively with their families, the problems of the proposed new land tenure system were not necessarily glaringly obvious.

The marginalization of gender issues which characterized the mainstream Tanzanian land debate was not challenged by women's groups. They proved incapable of launching a critique of the reforms or of proposing a manifesto of demands. Rather than setting the policy agenda, they reacted to proposals. Rather than presenting detailed analyses of the issues at stake, they limited themselves to an instrumental approach to legislation.[12]

The struggle for statutory spousal co-ownership in Uganda In Uganda, as in Tanzania, women's groups became involved in the land debate at a relatively late stage of the reform process. More recently, however, they have been thoroughly engaged in lobbying on land matters. Ugandan women's groups began to lobby for the inclusion of statutory spousal co-ownership of family land during debates on the draft land bill which was passed into law in 1998. During the drafting of the land bill, many prominent women politicians and members of non-governmental organizations agreed on the need for spousal co-ownership and took part in lobbying to achieve it. Their first defeat occurred in 1998 after they had drafted a provision for co-ownership with the objective of having it included in the Land Act.[13] The amendment was tabled in Parliament on 25 June 1998. It was moved by the MP Miriam Matembe, debated and adopted by the floor and summed up by the speaker. Women's groups congratulated themselves on the clause's inclusion in the new land law. But when the Land Act was published a few days later, 'there was no trace of this amendment ... women MPs and women in civil society ... were told that there had been procedural irregularities in the way they had tabled the amendment which then disqualified it. In the end, the President admitted that he had intervened personally to delete the amendment.'[14]

A series of further promises to reintroduce the amendment

emanated from the Ugandan government but were also broken and, in 2000, it was announced by the cabinet that, in its judgment, the clause should now be diverted to the domestic relations bill.[15] The domestic relations bill represents the first time since the 1960s that there has been an attempt to achieve a radical overhaul of Ugandan family law. It dates from 1994 when the Attorney-General and the Minister of Justice requested the Law Commission to recommend new family law provisions. The domestic relations bill was completed in 1999 but its progress through Parliament has been severely delayed. Gender progressive groups vigorously and consistently resisted the suggestion that they should not throw their lot in with this legislation. There were two reasons for their strong preference for an amendment to the Land Act 1998, one strategic and the other symbolic. First, the difficulties surrounding the domestic relations bill quite understandably caused women's groups to doubt whether it would ever be approved by Parliament. Controversy had surrounded the bill's recognition of an offence of marital rape and provisions for no-fault divorce, both of which were heavily criticized by male members of Parliament. The domestic relations bill appeared to be in peril and for strategic reasons; therefore, proponents of the co-ownership clause were fearful that their proposal would suffer a similar fate.

There was, second, an important symbolic reason for preferring the clause to be included in the Land Act 1998. Women's groups clearly wished for gender progressive measures to appear in 'hard' land law rather than to be relegated to what is perceived as the softer world of family law. Resistance to the notion that women's land rights were a matter of family law formed an important part of the campaign. The attempt to contain the issue of women's land rights within the scope of family laws would not be without precedent. The Tanzanian land reform process was notable for failing to address the need for women's independent land rights. The Commission of Inquiry into Land

Matters (the 'Shivji Commission') dealt with issues of women's land rights in an extremely brief section of its report, arguing that the issue was outside its terms of reference; that it amounted to a problem of unequal succession; and that it should be taken up by the Law Reform Commission. Elsewhere, I have argued that this was an unnecessarily restrictive interpretation of the Commission's terms of reference. Rather than taking seriously the demand for women's independent land rights, the suggestion that this was a matter for the Law Reform Commission implied that women relate to land not as farmers and workers but only as wives, daughters and mothers. Given the history of gender and land reform in East Africa, an amendment to *land* laws, specifically the Uganda Land Act 1998, was clearly perceived to be an important symbolic struggle.

Since it first began to be voiced, the demand for statutory co-ownership of land in Uganda has met with explicit and concerted opposition from male parliamentarians and others. They have played an important role in the land debate and the reasons for their opposition to spousal co-ownership have been widely publicized. These include fears that a change in the law would provide women with an incentive to engage in serial marriage, treating the institutions simply as a means to acquire land. Male parliamentarians openly voiced such concerns, which had the merit of provoking fierce media debate as well as affording advocates of statutory spousal co-ownership opportunities to counter such perceptions. A feature of the Ugandan spousal co-ownership debate that has been much neglected, however, is the lobbying activities of commercial lenders. Operating in a far from transparent manner, commercial lenders exerted pressure on MPs to oppose the co-ownership proposal. I will argue in Chapter 6 that the lobbying activities of commercial lenders will play a prominent role in the coming years and that their involvement in land relations will be crucial in a privatized, individualized land market. For the purposes of this case study, however, it is important to stress that, despite their reluctance openly to debate the issue of spousal co-ownership of family land, it is clear that commercial lenders did influence the land reform agenda in Uganda. I would suggest that their opposition and the lobbying activities in which they engaged behind the scenes played a significant part in shoring up suspicion of the proposed amendment to the Land Act 1998 among male parliamentarians.

Given the disappointments and defeats faced by women's groups, it was not surprising that Parliament's eventual approval of the co-ownership amendment in June 2003 was hailed as an important victory for gender progressive groups. Shortly afterwards, however, it was announced that the president had refused to sign the new amendment into law. While Uganda has shown itself willing to adopt equality provisions in international conventions such as CEDAW, it is clear that the state cannot be relied upon to implement these objectives beyond the level of rhetoric. The Ugandan experience illustrates that consideration of, and scepticism about, third world women's relationship to the state and to international law remains as relevant as ever.[16]

In an attempt to protest against the government's actions in blocking the inclusion of the co-ownership amendment in the Land Act 1998, gender progressive groups sought help from the British Department for International Development (DfID). DfID was closely involved in promoting, funding and overseeing the introduction of Uganda's new land law. For example, the process of drafting Uganda's land laws had been the responsibility of a technical legal consultant funded by DfID.[17] Furthermore, as I discussed in Chapter 3, continued bilateral aid from Britain was required to implement the new land laws, set up the vast new machinery of land administration required by the Act and train the bureaucrats who were expected to run it. The project to do this was entitled the Securing Sustainable Livelihoods through Land Tenure Reform Project (widely known as the Land Act Implementation Project) and it was to be overseen by British technical advice.[18] DfID was thus an extremely powerful actor on the Ugandan land scene as it was in many African countries.

When, in 1999, the Speaker pronounced his judgment that in order for spousal co-ownership to become law the house would need to pass new amending legislation, gender progressive groups relayed the news to DfID. It, in turn, announced that it was making it a condition of further funding under the Land Act Implementation Project that the 'lost clause' be reintroduced to Parliament by the end of the year.[19] The Ugandan government ignored this condition and did not reintroduce the clause for discussion. In a betrayal of the cause of gender progressive groups, DfID chose not to utilize its considerable influence to the good and did not press the point.

The experience of Ugandan land reform provides an illustration of the limits of African governments' commitment to a gender progressive normative order and of the acquiescence of bilateral donors in this. The story of efforts to achieve gender equality in land relations in Uganda is replete with disappointments, broken promises and betrayals. In common with many African countries Uganda, unable to step aside and avoid the neo-liberal juggernaut, found itself the proud owner of a new set of land laws. What follows is an attempt to understand its response to finding itself in this position. Unable to avoid the liberalization of land, and perhaps alert to the dangers of this new commodification for women, gender progressive groups began to seek ways to contain, if not to resist, these new dangers.

The alienation of family land, on which women live and grow food but over which they rarely exercise control, appeared at first to be the key concern of gender progressive groups and feminist politicians. As is apparent from the World Bank's global land policy explored in Chapter 3, on the macroeconomic plane the liberalization of land markets is intricately linked with wider institutional reforms. The key questions facing gender progressive groups thus seemed to be: how best might we respond to the threat to women of losing the land on which they and their families are dependent for their livelihoods? Having lost (without much of a fight, it must be conceded) the initial battle over commodification, their attention strayed from political economy to the law. A further structural explanation can also be offered. Uganda is remarkable among African countries for the number of women lawyers it possesses. Among these lawyers, many wield influence and power as members of the urban, middle-class elite who found and control gender progressive groups. In these circumstances, it was not surprising that the struggle into which these groups poured their energy was not the wider issue of the liberalization of the economy and with it the land; instead, as the discussion which follows shows, the law itself became a site of critique. An amendment of existing land legislation came to be fetishized. It is in this context that spousal co-ownership became a key demand and consent a key juridical notion. The largely absent battles over commodification before 1998 has thus been replaced more recently by skirmishes over the content of the law.

Since the late 1980s, there has been a proliferation of non-governmental organizations focusing on issues of land reform in Africa. Such groups have rarely contested the emphasis placed by international donors and financial institutions on technical legal solutions to the problems of land relations.[20] Civil society groups, dependent on external donor funding (and the annual production of progress reports) for their existence, have been stringently self-limiting. Law reform has been a key objective and one which they have sought to achieve by lobbying fellow members of the urban, middle-class elite. On occasion they have had the sturdy support of their external patrons, although they have also had to become accustomed to being let down in this regard. A multitude of possible alliances, with trade unions to take just one example, have been left unexplored.

The key anxiety for those non-governmental organizations that focus on gender issues is that there is likely to be an increase in disputes concerning the sale and mortgaging of land. In particular, in coming years women will be forced to try to defend against institutional lenders the land on which they depend for a livelihood. As I will show in Chapter 6, there is every reason to expect that such cases will become a central feature of the African political, economic and judicial landscape as landholders are encouraged to raise loans using their homes and farms as collateral. Formal credit institutions, that is commercial banks, will come to play an increasingly important role in land relations. The task of gender progressive groups, as they have seen it, has been to search for legal provisions which protect women's interests in primary family land. In particular, there has been an apparent concern to guard against the alienation, mortgaging or leasing of such land without a wife's prior consent. Gender progressive groups and feminist politicians in a number of African countries have lobbied for various legal mechanisms to achieve such protection.[21] These have ranged from the insertion of consent clauses into new land laws to schemes for statutory spousal co-ownership of family land.

Since it first began to be made in 1998, the demand for co-ownership in Uganda has met with concerted opposition from male parliamentarians and others. Nevertheless, women's groups took the view that the consent clause contained in the Land Act 1998 did not provide adequate protection for women. Instead, they consistently demanded that a scheme for statutory co-ownership of primary family land be passed into law. Uganda has taken the lead in debating the most effective statutory provisions by which to protect women's interests in land. It has to a large extent determined the terms in which similar discussions will be conducted in the rest of Africa. I would argue, however, that women's groups have been thrown back on the problematic notion of consent as a consequence of the wider failure to resist liberalization and thus secure a more abiding victory for women and men's secure rights to land. Far from being the endpoint in the struggle for women's

111

land rights, the achievement of spousal co-ownership should be viewed only as the foundation for future struggle. I therefore foresee a central role for consent as a juridical concept in the coming years. We would do well, in exploring current struggles to claim women's land rights, to remember that juridical notions such as consent have come to prominence because of an earlier important defeat. Had Uganda and other African countries been able to resist the liberalization of land tenure and the commodification of land, the threat of transferability of land would not now be hanging over many parts of the continent. Consent would not have attained this prominent role. Central to the story told in this chapter, therefore, is an originary story of defeat. The contestation over the workings of co-ownership and the meaning of consent which we will witness in coming years will be a permanent reminder of the inability of the global south to resist political and economic prescriptions to commodify land.

The Ugandan experience of claiming women's land rights was informed by an instrumentalist view of law. This attempted explicitly to link the claim for legal change to allow spousal co-ownership with development. Although at first sight it appeared that it was fear of the new macroeconomic climate that drove the demand for co-ownership, a closer reading of the activities of women's groups suggests that, in reality, this was if anything a secondary concern. Rather, adopting and adapting the mythical claims of the World Bank to their own ends, gender progressive groups spoke the language of economic growth, poverty alleviation and access to capital. In short, in staking their claims in terms of law reform they had recourse to the outlook and objectives of law in development, revived this time in a neo-liberal guise. But they also sought to determine the legal sphere in which they wished their claims to be heard. Land law, not family law, was the ground on which Africa's entrepreneurial spirit was to be set free. Gender progressive groups sought not to challenge and contest the construction of economic man but instead to invite support for economic woman. They sought a place in the world of hard land law and in the masculine world of the market. Alternative visions of land which expressed values different from this did not find a voice. Such meanings have been articulated by those excluded from the formation of the World Bank's global land policy[22] or from national processes of land reform.[23] As I show below, they have also been voiced by emerging rural movements in Africa.

I would argue that gender progressive groups in Uganda did little to contest the wider neo-liberal project within which women's land rights formed only one important element. Indeed, as I have attempted to demonstrate, they took as their own the language of economic development promoted by advocates of liberalization. In staking their claims for spousal co-ownership, therefore, they did not challenge the wider macroeconomic pressures for land and credit markets but sought to press home their demands precisely by harnessing that wider macroeconomic climate. Nowhere were the dangers entailed in linking a family's primary asset and means of livelihood to commercial loans and business enterprise pointed out.

There is of course a rich irony, never explored, in the fact that statutory co-ownership, far from securing women's rights, will in all probability lead to an increase in the use of family land as collateral. Statutory co-ownership may be said to make the work of commercial lenders, and the solicitors on whom they rely, a great deal easier. The Bankers' Association of Uganda had already complained consistently of the conveyancing burdens imposed on them by the consent clause in section 40 of the Land Act 1998 (we might describe this as the original consent clause). Their opposition to the consent requirement was vocal: they objected to having to carry out inquiries and institute checks to ascertain whether adequate consents to loan transactions had been obtained.[24] It is arguable that the new co-ownership provision should therefore be a cause for celebration. Statutory co-ownership will in fact reduce the conveyancing work which must be done before a loan is released. The presumption that all land is co-owned will lower lending risks because banks would be alert to the need to acquire the consent of the other spouse. Before the achievement of statutory co-ownership, the original consent clause entailed a greater risk for the bank, and higher transaction costs, because of the more complicated inquiries which had to be made of borrowers about the possible interests of other individuals.

The reality of this fact has already been noted. Co-ownership 'has the potential to strengthen the credit market by providing statutory regulation in an area which is already of concern for the banking sector'.[25] It may well ease the working of the credit market and lead to increased certainty in the commercial lending sector. It would of course be entirely valid for it to have been introduced into law for this reason. However, advocates of women's land rights need to ask whether the facilitation of the credit market was in fact their intention and whether this will serve to improve or hamper women's access to land. The irony of what has occurred in Uganda lies in the possibility – which it will no doubt take some years and a few cases in the law courts to appreciate – that the struggle for statutory co-ownership may in fact facilitate a rampant commercial lending market which will deprive women of the land on which they have long relied for their livelihoods.

Ideologies and tactics of rural movements

In a comprehensive study of rural movements, their strategies and their potential as opponents of neo-liberalism, Moyo and Yeros have sought to focus on issues of agency, highlighting the 'conscious attempt by the rural poor to influence the state and market through land occupations, and thereby lead the way through the various steps: they self-select as beneficiaries, they select the land, they acquire it de facto, and then await their legal formalization by the state. This may indeed follow, or it may not.'[26]

This important account of rural movements acknowledges the engagement of rural movements with the juridical sphere by suggesting that they have adopted a sceptical stance in relation to the content and processes of state law. Holding themselves at a distance to the law, they have sought to exercise their own agency by themselves identifying those with land needs, by locating suitable land and by moving to acquire it. Recognition by the state of the rights over land thereby acquired, should it follow, is treated as a secondary concern. Moyo and Yeros's main focus is on the political significance and potential of emergent social movements organizing around land issues. Although their observation on the distance of rural movements from the law is important, legal strategies are not the focal point of their discussion.

Focusing specifically on the significance of legal struggles, Meszaros's study of one of the world's most prominent social movements, Brazil's Movimento dos Trabalhadores Rurais Sem Terra (Movement of Landless Rural Workers or MST), provides an analysis of the significance of law in building and sustaining social struggles and in so doing has drawn attention to the severe limitations of formal legal processes and institutions.[27] Houtzager has also studied the MST by focusing on the movement's emerging legal strategies. He has shown that although the movement does not possess any standing to initiate law cases, it has become involved in the juridical sphere as a result of civil and criminal cases brought against it. Houtzager shows that this 'reactive juridical mobilisation ... has grown increasingly sophisticated'. For Houtzager, the MST have seized such opportunities to promote a redefinition of property rights and it is significant that this has been achieved at the same moment that international institutions such as the World Bank have been engaged in 'globalizing a new "classic" interpretation of liberal property rights'.[28] Furthermore, for Houtzager:

Five

The MST's juridical mobilisation ... sheds light on some of the ways in which social movements can use the law to create countervailing possibilities to the particular 'liberal' property regime that is being globalised from above. It has played a substantial role in altering a highly exclusionary legality by compelling public authorities to implement existing agrarian reform legislation and by helping to create and institutionalise novel interpretations of the social function of property.[29]

Bernstein has also highlighted the differences between rural social movements' outlook on property rights and those of powerful institutions at the international level. The direct action strategies of rural movements indicates a 'strongly oppositional ideological stance' that employs political tactics that do not correspond with the clear 'aversion to confiscation and desire for consensus of market-friendly "new wave" reform' that characterizes the thinking of bilateral donors and international financial institutions.[30] In spite of the diversity of global rural movements organizing to challenge the unequal distribution of land, their common outlook on the state is summed up in the words of a leader of Brazil's MST: 'We have always been told that agrarian reform is a good idea in principle, but the *conjuntura*, or present moment, isn't right. Well, we make the *conjuntura* right.'[31] This is not to suggest that no connections exist between the activities of rural movements and policy developments at state and international levels. Moyo and Yeros have also argued that 'the low-profile (illegal "squatting") tactic is also known to exercise influence over the policy process, but in a much more diffuse and contingent manner'.[32] Bernstein makes a similar observation in relation to the MST in Brazil arguing that 'the introduction of World Bank and USAID land-titling and similar "new wave" programmes ... seems to have been accelerated to counter the successes of the MST'.[33]

Conclusion

Cultural globalization has created and sustained a close tie between elite women in the global south and their northern sponsors. The local wing of this transnational bourgeoisie has been less alert to local needs and debates than to the issues occupying their international peers. This in part explains the remarkably delayed participation of African women's groups in land reform debates. In the face of economic globalization, neither national governments nor the bilateral donors on whom they have had to rely to fund the extensive land reform programmes of the last two decades have been influenced by the objectives of gender progressive international law. African governments have done little to ensure the promotion of gender progressive laws and have most often taken action instead to block progress on women's land rights. Despite the considerable influence they wield, bilateral donors have not opposed this neglect of women's rights. The interests of bilateral donors in the opening up of African economies, including the liberalization of land, have taken precedence over any commitment to progress on issues of gender equality. It is also suggested that, at the international level, institutions such as the World Bank have singularly failed to acknowledge gender progressive international law instruments. Indeed, as I argue in the next chapter, the global land agenda of the World Bank is parasitic upon, and threatens to worsen, unequal rural gender relations.

African states are experiencing unprecedented pressure to privatize land. Economic globalization has opened their economy to outside influence and has meant that despite signing up to the feminist normative project, by ratifying international law instruments such as CEDAW for example, the fate of such important national resources as land has been far more influenced by powerful economic actors such as international financial institutions, donors, property-owning men and commercial bankers who on the evidence do not share similar goals of gender equity.

Presenting two case studies, I have shown in this chapter that gender progressive groups have remained within the magnetic field of the law and have proved reluctant to challenge the promotion of law as a means to alter land relations. These groups failed to contest the trend for the commodification of land and to offer alternatives to the language of formalization and the market. Instead, as the Ugandan example illustrates, they sought to employ and harness this language themselves in order to make the case for women's access to land. I have argued that gender progressive groups thereby reinforced the network of land law reform and have in fact formed an important element of the network.

I have also argued in this chapter that the emergence and growing profile of rural social movements suggests that we may be witnessing an important contrast to this approach. Recognizing, as Bernstein has urged,[34] the many contradictions and tensions that characterize rural movements, I have argued that they nevertheless provide an important counter to law's dominance in the field of land reform and more broadly of development. Accounts of established landless peoples' movements such as Brazil's MST suggest that while rural movements will engage with law when necessary, and score substantial successes by redefining property rights and introducing new ideas such as the need to acknowledge the social function of property, they have resisted the dominance of the law and legal discourse as the means to bring about economic and social development. The oppositional politics of rural movements – in both conceptual and tactical terms – has served to throw into relief the state-centred and consensus-driven approach of gender progressive groups.

Notes

1 See B. Agarwal, *A Field of One's Own: Gender and Land Rights in South Asia* (Cambridge: Cambridge University Press, 1994), p. 4.

2 See <www.tgnp.org> (accessed December 2005).

3 For a discussion of the different types of women's groups in Tanzania, see A. M. Tripp, 'Rethinking Civil Society: Gender

Implications in Contemporary Tanzania', in J. W. Harbeson, D. Roth-child and N. Chazan (eds), *Civil Society and the State in Africa* (London: Lynne Rienner, 1994).

4 J. Sayers, N. Redclift and M. Evans (eds), *Engels Revisited: New Feminist Essays* (London: Tavistock, 1987); and M. Molyneux, 'Socialist Societies Old and New: Progress Towards Women's Emancipation', *Feminist Review*, 8 (1981), pp. 1–34.

5 See Agarwal, *A Field of One's Own*, p. 4.

6 Tanzania Gender Networking Programme, *Gender Profile of Tanzania* (Dar es Salaam: TGNP, 1993).

7 See Tanzania Women Lawyers' Association, *Report of the Proceedings and Recommendations of a Consultative Women's Workshop on the Draft Bill for the Basic Land Act*, held at the Russian Cultural Centre, Dar es Salaam, 3–5 March 1997.

8 M. K. Rwebangira and H. H. Sheikh, 'Critical Review of the Draft Bill for the Land Act from Women's Perspective', in Tanzania Women Lawyers' Association, *Report ... on the Draft Bill for the Basic Land Act*.

9 See I. Maro, 'Women Lawyers Want Land Bill Amended', *Daily Nation*, 5 March 1997.

10 'Convention on the Elimination of All Forms of Discrimination Against Women', reprinted in P. R. Ghandhi, *International Human Rights Documents* (London: Blackstone Press, 1995), pp. 82–90.

11 H. Pietila and J. Vickers, *Making Women Matter: The Role of the United Nations* (London: Zed Books, 1990); and A. Byrne, 'Toward More Effective Enforcement of Women's Human Rights Through the Use of International Human Rights Procedures', in R. Cook (ed.), *Human Rights of Women: National and International Perspectives* (Philadelphia: University of Pennsylvania, 1994).

12 For a more detailed discussion of the Tanzanian land reform debate, see A. Manji, 'Gender and the Politics of the Land Tenure Reform Process in Tanzania', in *Journal of Modern African Studies*, 36 (4) (1998); and, for a response to my critique, D. Tsikata, 'Securing Women's Interests within Land Tenure Reforms: Recent Debates in Tanzania', in *Journal of Agrarian Change*, 3 (1 & 2) (2003), pp. 149–83. See also A. Whitehead and D. Tsikata, 'Policy Discourses on Women's Land Rights in Sub-Saharan Africa: The Implications of the Re-turn to the Customary', *Journal of Agrarian Change*, 3 (1 & 2) (2003), pp. 67–112.

13 H. Busingye, 'Lobbying and Advocacy on Women's Land Rights: The Experience of the Uganda Land Alliance', in M. Rugadya and H. Busingye (eds), *Gender Perspectives in the Land Reform Process in Uganda* (Kampala: Uganda Land Alliance, 2002), p. 19.

14 A. M. Goetz, 'No Shortcuts to Power: Constraints on Women's Political Effectiveness in Uganda', *Journal of Modern African Studies*, 40 (4) (2002), pp. 549–75, 564; A. M. Tripp, 'Conflicting Visions of

Community and Citizenship: Women's Rights and Cultural Diversity in Uganda', in M. Molyneux and S. Razavi (eds), *Gender, Justice, Development, and Rights* (Oxford: Oxford University Press, 2002). For an account of the work of women's groups to have the clause included in the new law, and the bizarre circumstances surrounding its being dropped from the Land Act 1998, see the chapter entitled 'A Moment of Reality: The Land Act 1998' in M. Matembe, *Gender, Politics and Constitution Making in Uganda* (Kampala: Fountain Publishers, 2002); J. Asiimwe, 'Making Women's Land Rights a Reality in Uganda: Advocacy for Co-ownership by Spouses', *Yale Human Rights and Development Law Journal*, 4 (2001), pp. 173–89.

15 See Goetz, 'No Shortcuts to Power'.

16 A. Stewart, 'Should Women Give Up On the State? An African Perspective', in S. Rai and G. Lievesley (eds), *Women and the State: International Perspectives* (London: Taylor and Francis, 1996), pp. 23–44.

17 A. Manji, 'Cause and Consequence in Law and Development', *Journal of Modern African Studies*, 43 (1) (2005), pp. 119–38.

18 See A. Stewart, 'Juridifying Gender Justice: From Global Rights to Local Justice', in H. Hatchard and A. Perry-Kessaris (eds), *Law and Development: Facing Complexity in the 21st Century* (London: Cavendish, 2003), pp. 36–54.

19 P. McAuslan, *Bringing the Law Back In: Essays in Land, Law and Development* (London: Ashgate, 2003).

20 World Bank, *The World Bank and Technical Legal Assistance*, Report No. 414 (Washington, DC: World Bank, 1995).

21 A. M. Tripp, 'The Politics of Autonomy and Cooption in Africa', *Journal of Modern African Studies*, 39 (2001), pp. 101–28.

22 See, for example, Open Letter to the World Bank on Land Policy Consultation: An African Appeal, a document signed by a number of South African organizations, including the National Land Committee; Rural Development Services Network; Landless People's Movement; Transkei Land Service Organisation; and Southern Africa Network on Land. Available at <www.nlc.co.za/pubs/wbopenletter02.htm> (accessed December 2005). For more detailed discussion, see Chapter 3.

23 I. G. Shivji, 'Land: The Terrain of Democratic Struggle', *Change*, 5 (1997), p. 77.

24 L. A. Wily et al., *Impact of Spousal Co-ownership of the Primary Household Property: A Short Study Conducted for the Land Act Implementation Project* (Kampala: Ministry of Water, Lands and Environment, 2000).

25 Ibid., p. 1.

26 S. Moyo and P. Yeros (eds), *Reclaiming the Land: The Resurgence of Rural Movements in Africa, Asia and Latin America* (London: Zed Books, 2005), p. 53.

27 G. Meszaros, 'Taking the Land into Their Hands: The Landless Workers' Movement and the Brazilian State', *Journal of Law and Society*, 27 (4) (2000), pp. 517–41.

28 P. Houtzager, 'The Movement of the Landless (MST) and the Juridical Field in Brazil', *Institute of Development Studies Working Paper*, 248 (Sussex: Institute of Development Studies, 2005).

29 Ibid.

30 See H. Bernstein, 'Land Reform: Taking a Long(er) View', *Journal of Agrarian Change*, 2 (4) (2002), pp. 433–63, 456.

31 S. Banford and J. Rocha, *Cutting the Wire: The Story of the Landless Movement in Brazil* (London: Latin American Bureau, 2002).

32 Ibid., p. 53.

33 Bernstein, 'Land Reform', p. 456. See also Banford and Rocha, *Cutting the Wire.*

34 H. Bernstein, 'Rural Land and Land Conflicts in Sub-Saharan Africa', in Moyo and Yeros (eds), *Reclaiming the Land*, pp. 67–101.

Contesting law?

6 The future of land relations

The changes in land relations that have characterized the last two decades in Africa will have a profound impact in coming years and will raise a number of difficult new issues. I argue in what follows that there are three important aspects of land relations that will require further research and demand political attention. First, it is likely that we will witness the continuation of the problems of implementation that have already begun to be experienced. The problems associated with implementing vast and complex new land laws may mean that many disputes over land, as well as regular dealings in land, encounter a legal vacuum. Second, I identify a likely worsening of women's position and of gender relations more generally as a consequence of the promotion of formalization of land tenure and of formal rural credit markets. I explore the gender implications of the influential World Bank policy research report and show that if the situation it envisages comes to pass, women's unpaid labour will be put under increasing strain in coming years. I argue that the promotion of formal rural credit will have far-reaching consequences for women who will be exposed to greater risk of debt and dispossession than ever before. Third, I show that although it has received little attention to date, the involvement of commercial lenders in the land law reform process suggests that they may seek to play a prominent role in land matters in the future. It is important to be alert to the lobbying power they assert, and to the likelihood that they will receive the enthusiastic backing of national governments, bilateral donors and international financial institutions. Related to this, I argue, the African judiciary will find itself at the forefront of land relations in coming years. Called upon to mediate between the needs of landowners and occupiers on the one hand and the demands of commercial lenders for certainty and for low risks in lending on the other, the judiciary will come to play a key role. It is not yet clear what their response will be, but case law in this area from other jurisdictions, such as that relating to mortgages secured on matrimonial homes, does not give cause for optimism.

Problems of implementation

In his account of his work as a technical legal consultant in the area of land law reform, McAuslan has identified implementation as an aspect of equity that is connected with 'the pursuit of fair and just land policies'. In relation to the Uganda's Land Act 1998 he relates:

> This story is a case study on the implementation of a new land law ... and how the best intentions of the Ministers and Parliament can be corrupted and subverted by bureaucrats ... land reform involves much more than land law reform ... It goes to the heart of governance and a failure to focus on that will likely undermine any good intentions to promote land reform.[1]

McAuslan provides a critical first-hand account of the problems encountered in Uganda, one which will 'be of interest to all those concerned with more than just the text of a new land law'.[2] Indeed, it is an account that should be read by anyone interested in the implementation of new laws in any sector.

By the end of the 1990s, when it became apparent that many countries in Africa would soon possess new land laws, the question of their implementation began to be discussed. References to the problems that were already being encountered became common.[3] However, the terms in which implementation has been understood and discussed have been limited. Problems of implementation are attended to only in so far as observers express fears about the workability of proposed bills or about newly approved legislation. It is widely assumed that where difficulties exist or can be foreseen, additional funding and enhanced training of those responsible for implementation will resolve them. As I demonstrated in Chapter 4, Coldham's analysis of the task of implementing the Uganda Land Act 1998 centres on the technical and administrative nature of the problem. The emphasis is on how to ensure that the administrative personnel responsible for the new legislation are adequately trained.[4] The process of implementation itself has remained neglected and little theorised. A vast literature, predominantly within political science and policy studies, which has sought to develop critical approaches to implementation has thus been overlooked.[5] This is all the more remarkable given the tradition of interdisciplinarity and of scepticism about the efficacy of using law to bring about social change which existed among scholars within the broad law in development movement.[6]

Worsening gender relations

The World Bank's Policy Research Report on land was discussed in Chapter 3. I would like to suggest here that its approach to gender will mean that, despite the World Bank's professed commitment to equality between men and women encapsulated in international law, its global land policy over the next decade will worsen rather than ameliorate women's social and economic position.

Two of the core ideas on which the World Bank's policy document is constructed merit a feminist critique. The Bank stresses the importance of promoting formal rural credit markets and links this to the use of efficient family labour. In the view of the Bank, owner-operated farms are more efficient and productive than those relying on waged labour. At the heart of agricultural productivity lies the notion of 'non-contractible labour'.[7] The Bank purports to use this term to describe family labour although in reality it is likely to mean the agricultural labour of women. Such labour is thought to be efficient for three main reasons.

First, and most obviously, such labour is unremunerated. Second, 'non-contractible labour incurs no supervision costs', and third, it provides a highly motivated labour force. These factors are said to give small farms a productivity advantage over larger operations which are dependent on waged labour.

The notion of women's unpaid labour remains at the heart of the Bank's plans for agricultural productivity. As it notes, 'family members ... can be employed without incurring hiring or search costs'.[8] The World Bank's assumption about the availability of non-contractible effort is extremely problematic. In promoting the idea of owner-operated farms, the Bank seeks to avoid the use of what it perceives to be expensive, inefficient and inflexible waged labour in agriculture. The employment contract is to be avoided in favour of non-contractible, flexible, willing and unpaid labour, that is, women's labour.

The idea of non-contractibility takes the private sphere of the household to be characterized by affective ties of community, which give rise to solidarity between individuals. In contrast, feminist theorists have revealed that the private sphere is often based on quasi-feudal domination and on coercion rather than freedom.[9] Central to the World Bank's idea of agricultural productivity is the assumption that women's household (and therefore agricultural) labour is freely available as an extension of their reproductive labour (under a figurative 'sexual contract').[10] The assumption appears to be that women will demand less in terms of wages and conditions than waged labour.

Drawing on the debates surrounding feminist demands that women should be paid for housework,[11] it is possible to assess the impact on agricultural productivity of women being remunerated for their household and agricultural labour. Labour constitutes the greatest cost on small farms and it is therefore clear that if family labour were to be waged, this would constitute a cost rather than a saving, reducing the productive and competitive advantage of the unit. The entire notion of the productive and competitive advantage of owner-operated farms over those dependent on waged labour is founded on the availability of the labour of women which is taken to be free, flexible and willing.

There has long been a considerable literature available, much of it dealing specifically with the third world, which has revealed the ways in which the family 'functions as an ideological and economic site of oppression'.[12] The availability of women's unwaged labour within the family, which is closely coupled to male control over women's reproductive capacity, has been the central focus of these feminist analyses.[13] The World Bank takes the household as its smallest unit of analysis[14] and in so doing conflates the interests of its individual members. This neglects a vast body of established literature that has problematized the household and shown how the interests of its members cannot be assumed to be identical.[15] There is a presumption of the coercive power of the male head of the household which is hidden by the idea of family members' motivation to increase agricultural productivity. The World Bank is at the very least taking for granted and at the most advocating feudal family relations. The patriarchal power of kinship structures appears to be a prerequisite for the World Bank's plans for increased agricultural productivity in the developing world.[16]

Given its explicit attempt to link land policy to poverty reduction, the World Bank should at the very least be alert to the likelihood that its proposals will have an adverse impact on women. Its failure to address this issue suggests the tacit collusion of the World Bank in women's oppression. The notion of productivity advantage, and its founding assumption of women's motivation, promises to do a great deal to embed the very patriarchal, feudal gender relations that the World Bank professes elsewhere to be committed to alleviating. Poverty alleviation and economic development clearly require, for the Bank, the full disciplinary power of patriarchy and the hidden coercion and often outright violence on which it depends for its authority.

Arguably the most important aspect of the World Bank's land policy is its promotion of the idea of rural credit markets. According to the Bank, policies that make it possible to use land as a means to access credit turn it from a dead asset into an economically viable resource resulting in what the Report perceives to be major equity benefits.[17] The inability of households to access credit using their land as collateral is said to have an adverse affect on the emergence and working of rural credit markets. Economic growth as a whole is held back if rural land is allowed to remain a 'dead asset'. For the Bank, the acquisition of secure tenure rights is desirable because it increases the supply of credit from formal credit institutions using land as collateral.[18]

The Bank's land policy also envisages that credit will allow households to engage in productive entrepreneurial activities. It also hopes that credit will enable the household to invest money in social expenditure on public goods such as schooling and healthcare. The explicit assumption is that improvements in credit markets and in agricultural production will contribute to overall economic growth. It is important to locate this idea in the wider work of the World Bank and its development thinking. The World Bank's role in the privatization of public goods is well known. In the 1980s, the introduction of user fees in African hospitals and the imposition of school fees (both services which were hitherto provided by the state at no cost to the user) fundamentally altered the economic and social landscape.[19] These initiatives reduced the role of the state and created a market in public goods. Seen in this light, the World Bank can now be said to be encouraging the poorest and most vulnerable to exploit what is often their sole productive asset, their land, to raise credit by which to pay for previously public goods such as schools, hospitals and roads. The promotion of rural credit to pay for public goods has at its base the exploitation of women's unpaid labour.[20]

Looking into the future, it is also possible to predict with some accuracy the consequences of this neo-liberal economic model, which seeks to provide security of tenure precisely in order to encourage the use of land as collateral for loans. Reliance on credit secured on the family home and utilized to foster small business enterprise characterized Britain in the 1970 and 1980s. The encouragement of owner-occupied housing went hand-in-hand with the development of small owner-run businesses. It is precisely this idea that is appearing in the African context in the efforts by the World Bank and their allies in the British Department for International Development to encourage rural credit and non-farm entrepreneurial activities. An inevitable result of encouraging formal rural credit will be that law courts will come increasingly to be faced with cases involving lenders, borrowers and family land. As Fehlberg has pointed out, the steep rise in English law cases involving surety wives – between 1986 and 1994, the Court of Appeal heard eleven cases on this issue – can be traced directly to government policy in the preceding years which sought to encourage the establishment of small businesses using the family home as security. Furthermore, if the productivity advantage of small farms is based on women's labour, and that productivity advantage is itself the reason for encouraging the use of land as collateral, then given the well-documented role of women as the primary workers on the land,[21] it is not an exaggeration to suggest that it will ultimately be women's labour on the land that services rural debt and underpins economic development.[22]

Those employed to work on gender issues within the World Bank were curiously silent during both the formulation of the Bank's land policy document and the brief consultation process on the draft reports. According to the World Bank's Operational Manual, it 'aims to integrate gender considerations in its country assistance program'. Given this professed aim, one would have expected to hear feminist critiques of the draft land policy from within the institutions, if not attempts to alter the course of the World Bank's thinking.[23] It is somewhat surprising that the promotion of rural credit and non-contractible labour has not been challenged. It is clear that those employed by the World Bank itself to work on gender issues have not questioned the land policy's basic assumptions.

Whether this failure is explained by a lack of integrated thinking at the Bank[24] or is better understood as the result of lack of consultation on the draft documents, it is striking that the 'women in development' efforts of the 1970s appear to have had no impact on the work of the World Bank.[25] The land policy gives the distinct impression that the institution has stubbornly refused to be influenced by many years of feminist engagement in gender issues at the international level.

The role of commercial lenders and the judiciary

The role played by commercial lenders in the land reform process has received no attention from either academic commentators or policy-makers until now and yet it is clear that bankers' organizations have had a central place in determining the shape and content of Africa's new land laws. The liberalization of land markets and the promotion of formal credit provide unprecedented opportunities for commercial lenders in Africa. Their lobbying activities have already had a powerful impact as they have tried to ensure that new land laws do not increase the risks entailed in lending. They have been particularly active in lobbying against the inclusion in the law of provisions that seek to protect women in the family home, for example, by requiring a spouse's informed consent to land transactions to be acquired. Reports emanating from some African countries suggest that the concerns of commercial lenders have been taken up by politicians.[26] It is likely that they will continue to exert influence in the future. Given the lobbying power available to institutional lenders and the domestic and international interest in their growth, it can also be expected that they will vigorously resist attempts to develop mechanisms to protect weaker parties in land transactions. Connected to this is the part that will come to be played by the African judiciary. It may be that, over time, the promotion of rural credit will receive concerted backing from international donors and African governments. Might it be the case that in a few years' time, the judiciary will be seeking ways to fulfil the demands of commercial lenders for certainty in lending?

It might be argued that the means to counter such risks is to strengthen women's position through law, for example by ensuring that they must consent to loan transactions by their husbands. To take the case of Tanzania, the Land Acts 1999 make co-spousal registration and titling of customary rights possible. This is to be done by village councils which constitute elected village governments and which do have mandatory female representation. However, a number of problems arise for women attempting to secure their position in this way. Most glaringly in the Tanzanian case, the Land Acts do not make it compulsory to record women's interest in land. Given problems of legal illiteracy, it is extremely unlikely that a woman would know of or be aware of how to go about registering her customary interest.[27] Even where a woman is in a strong position to register her interest, the fact that it is likely to be construed as a hostile act by her husband would provide a strong disincentive against doing so.[28] The likelihood of achieving legal protection for women must be severely in doubt given problems of illiteracy, ignorance of legal rights and the likelihood of corruption in land matters.

Indeed, even in circumstances where consent to land transactions is required, such as where a woman is legal co-owner of a property, the possibility of coercion to consent or deliberate concealment from a woman of the extent of her liability has been recognized by law courts.[29] In recent years English courts, for example, have attempted to deal with this problem by imposing an obligation on lenders to arrange to meet the wife independently from the husband, to ensure that she has fully understood the transaction, and to advise her to take independent legal advice.[30] Even so, it has been shown by analysis of relevant case law that 'creditor-sympathetic outcomes are the commonplace' and furthermore that '[t]hese are inevitable given the policy view that favours the continuance of the use of the family home as security for business loans'.[31]

This indicates that considerations of social policy are often aggravated by commercial considerations. In recent years we have already witnessed lending institutions resisting the imposition of legal provisions that increase the burden on them in acquiring adequate security for loans. In this context, it is doubtful whether commercial lenders can be relied upon to make adequate inquiries as to the interests of spouses. To keep down the costs of processing loans, it is likely that they will simply accept the husband's assurances that his wife has consented to the mortgage. It is also difficult to envisage commercial lenders being compelled by law to exercise adequate safeguards. This might be done, for example, by issuing statutory or judicial guidance to the effect that a spouse should be advised to seek separate legal guidance.[32] If this were made mandatory so that a failure to do so would render the loan void or voidable,[33] it is likely that institutional lenders would be more hesitant about becoming involved in land-related credit markets.

Even more problematic is the conveyancing burden which would be imposed on commercial lenders of ascertaining the marital status of co-habitees on land.[34] In cases where marriage certificates are not available, for example for customary marriages, it is difficult to see how a bank can be expected to corroborate the facts as presented by an applicant for a loan. In these circumstances it would be possible for a man to raise loans using land as collateral without the knowledge or consent of his wife. Given the lobbying power available to institutional lenders and the evident domestic and international support for their growth, it is probable that they will vigorously and successfully resist attempts to develop adequate mechanisms to protect the property interests of women.

Commercial lenders have actively sought to protect the neo-liberal thrust of land policy. An early example of this attempt was the lobbying activities of the Bankers' Association of Uganda against the statutory requirement to obtain the consent of spouses to the sale, leasing or mortgaging of land which was contained in the land bill.[35] It therefore came as little surprise when the Bankers' Association began to lobby parliamentarians against any provision which went still further by allowing the statutory co-ownership of family land as discussed in Chapter 5. Commercial lenders' complaints centred on the substantial increase in the risk to them which would be entailed in co-owner-ship, the perception that co-ownership would increase the risk to purchasers of land and thereby discourage land transactions and the argument that such a scheme would increase the burden on lenders of ascertaining whether consent has been properly acquired and add to the transaction costs associated with lend-ing.[36] In sum, the main thrust of the arguments presented by the Bankers' Association (in so far as they can be ascertained, given the less than public lobbying activities in which the association engaged) was that the proposals to introduce statutory co-owner-ship went against the grain of the Land Act 1998. The primary objective of that legislation was to encourage and stimulate a market in land. The proposal to introduce co-ownership was seen as a putting an unnecessary brake on this process by forcing commercial lenders to make adequate inquiries as to the occu-pancy and other rights of a spouse.

Notes

1 P. McAuslan, *Bringing the Law Back In: Essays in Land, Law and Development* (Aldershot: Ashgate, 2003), p. 310.

2 Ibid.

3 See S. Coldham, 'Land Reform and Customary Rights in Uganda', *Journal of African Law*, 44 (2000), pp. 65–77; Government of Uganda, *Report of the Land Act Implementation Study* (Kampala: Ministry of Lands, 1999); and R. Palmer, 'The Struggle Continues: Evolving Land Policy and Tenure Reforms in Africa – Recent Policy and

Implementation Processes', in C. Toulmin and J. Quan (eds), *Evolving Land Rights, Policy and Tenure in Africa* (London: International Institute for Environment and Development, 2000).

4 Coldham, 'Land Reform and Customary Rights', p. 76.

5 F. Rourke, *Bureaucracy, Politics and Public Policy* (Boston, MA: Little Brown, 1976); R. Nakamura and F. Smallwood, *The Politics of Policy Implementation* (New York: St Martin's Press, 1980); J. Pressman and A. Wildavsky, *Implementation* (Berkeley, CA: University of California Press, 1973); J. Sorg, 'A Typology of Implementation Behaviors of Street-Level Bureaucrats', *Policy Studies Review*, 2 (1983), pp. 391–406.

6 S. Adelman and A. Paliwala, 'Law and Development in Crisis', in S. Adelman and A. Paliwala (eds), *Law and Crisis in the Third World* (London: Hans Zell, 1993), pp. 1–26.

7 This term was employed in the first draft of the Policy Research Report and subsequently omitted. However, the idea of non-contractible labour continues to inform the World Bank in its land policy.

8 World Bank, *Policy Research Report: Land Policies for Growth and Poverty Reduction* (Oxford: Oxford University Press, 2003).

9 See S. M. Rai, *Gender and the Political Economy of Development* (Cambridge: Polity, 2002); N. Kabeer, 'Gender, Production and Well-Being: Rethinking the Household Economy', Paper No. 288 (Sussex: Institute of Development Studies, 1991); A. Sen, 'Gender and Cooperative Conflicts', in I. Tinker (ed.), *Persistent Inequalities* (Oxford: Oxford University Press, 1990); and L. Beneria, 'The Enduring Debate Over Unpaid Labour', *International Labour Review*, 138 (3) (1999), pp. 287–309.

10 C. Pateman, *The Sexual Contract* (Cambridge: Polity, 1998).

11 A. Oakley, *The Sociology of Housework* (Oxford: Blackwell, 1985); E. Mallos (ed.), *The Politics of Housework* (London: Allison and Busby, 1980). See also the discussion contained in M. Mies, *Patriarchy and Accumulation on a World Scale: Women in the International Division of Labour* (London: Zed Books, 1986).

12 C. Smart, *The Ties That Bind: Law, Marriage and the Reproduction of Patriarchal Relations* (London: Routledge and Kegan Paul, 1984).

13 R. McDonough and R. Harrison, 'Patriarchy and Relations of Production', in A. Kuhn and A. M. Wolpe (eds), *Feminism and Materialism* (London: Routledge and Kegan Paul, 1978); S. Rowbotham, *Women's Consciousness, Men's World* (London: Penguin, 1973).

14 For a discussion of this approach in the context of land tenure, see I. Yngstrom, 'Women, Wives and Land Rights in Africa: Situating Gender Beyond the Household in the Debate Over Land Policy and Changing Tenure Systems', *Oxford Development Studies*, 30 (2002), pp. 21–40.

15 J. I. Guyer, 'Household and Community in African Studies',

African Studies Review, 24 (1981), pp. 87–137; J. I. Guyer and P. E. Peters, 'Introduction: Conceptualising the Household: Issues of Theory and Policy in Africa', *Development and Change*, 18 (1987), pp. 197–213; B. Agarwal, *A Field of One's Own: Gender and Land Rights in South Asia* (Cambridge: Cambridge University Press, 1994). For a historical perspective, which provides an account of the interests of male clan elders in the creation of customary law and the consequences for women, see M. Chanock, *Law, Custom and Social Order* (Cambridge: Cambridge University Press, 1985).

16 This approach was manifest in the early initiatives of the World Bank and other development agencies aimed at women. For a discussion see, in particular, Rai, *Gender and the Political Economy of Development*, p. 58, in which Rai argues that 'Patriarchal and liberal discourses, at both national and international level, left unchallenged the question of gender relations in society, and often made these attendant upon a sexual division of labour and individual negotiation within the family.'

17 World Bank, *Policy Research Report: Land Policies for Growth and Poverty Reduction* (Oxford: Oxford University Press, 2003).

18 Ibid., pp. 8–9.

19 See, for example, J. Harrington, 'Privatising Scarcity: Civil Liability and Medical Practice in Tanzania', *Journal of African Law*, 42 (1998), pp. 147–71; also J. Harrington, 'Law and the Commodification of Health Care in Tanzania', *Law, Social Justice and Global Development Journal*, 2 (2003) (available at <www2.warwick.ac.uk/fac/soc/law/elj/lgd/2003_2/harrington/> (accessed December 2005).

20 See B. Fehlberg, *Sexually Transmitted Debt: Surety Experience and English Law* (Oxford: Clarendon, 1997).

21 J. Davison (ed.), *Agriculture, Women and Land: The African Experience* (London: Westview, 1988).

22 For an account of women's difficulties in retaining loans raised under micro-credit schemes, see A.-M. Goetz and R. S. Gupta, 'Who Takes the Credit? Gender, Power and Control Over Loan Use in Rural Credit Programmes in Bangladesh', *World Development*, 24 (1) (1996), pp. 45–64. See also J. Lairop-Fonderson, 'The Disciplinary Power of Micro-Credit: Examples from Kenya and Cameroon', in J. Parpart, S. Rai and K. Staudt (eds), *Rethinking Empowerment in a Global/Local World* (London: Routledge, 2002).

23 For an account of attempts by 'femocrats' within the World Bank to influence policy, see Rai, *Gender and the Political Economy of Development*.

24 R. Jahan, *The Elusive Agenda: Mainstreaming Women in Development* (London: Zed Books, 1995); and K. Staudt, 'The Uses and Abuses of Empowerment Discourse', in Parpart et al. (eds), *Rethinking Empowerment in a Global/Local World*.

25 See A. Bandarage, 'Women in Development: Liberalism, Marxism and Marxist Feminism', in *Development and Change*, 15 (1984), pp. 495–515, and A. Stewart, 'The Dilemmas of Law in Women's Development', in Adelman and Paliwala (eds), *Law and Crisis in the Third World*, pp. 219–42.

26 For an account of recent development in Kenya, see <www.nationmedia.com/eastafrican/current/Regional/Regional240520044.html> and <www.nationmedia.com/eastafrican/current/Opinion/Editorial240520042.html> (accessed December 2005)

27 In England and Wales, Lord Denning was particularly critical of the Matrimonial Homes Act 1967 (now the Family Law Act 1996) which required that a wife protect her statutory right of occupation of the family home by registration: 'She would never have heard of a Class F land charge; and she would not have understood it if she had' (*Williams and Glyn's Bank Ltd. v. Boland* [1979] Ch. 312 at 318 *per* Lord Denning).

28 M. P. Thomson, 'Monied Might or Social Justice? Mortgage Repossessions and the Protection of Occupiers', in F. Meisel and P. Cook (eds), *Property and Protection: Legal Rights and Restrictions* (Oxford: Hart Publishing, 2000), pp. 157–76.

29 On the concept of 'undue influence' see Thomson, 'Monied Might or Social Justice?' For a discussion of the approach of the German Federal Constitutional Court to inequalities of bargaining power within marriage, see P. Zumbansen, 'Public Values, Private Contracts and the Colliding Worlds of Family and Market: German Federal Constitutional Court, "Marital Agreement" Decisions of 6 February 2001 and 29 March 2001', *Feminist Legal Studies*, 11 (1) (2003), pp. 71–84.

30 Judicial guidance to this effect was issued in *Barclays Banks v. O'Brien* [1994] 1 A.C. 180 at 189–90 *per* Lord Browne-Wilkinson. For criticisms, see B. Fehlberg, *Sexually Transmitted Debt: Surety Experience and English Law* (Oxford: Oxford University Press, 1997). See also *Royal Bank of Scotland plc v. Etridge (No. 2)* [2001] 4 All E.R. 449 and, for discussion of the case, D. Morris, 'Surety Wives in the House of Lords: Time for Solicitors to "Get Real"?', *Feminist Legal Studies*, 11 (1) (2003), pp. 57–69.

31 See B. Fehlberg, 'The Husband, the Bank, the Wife and Her Signature – the Sequel', *Modern Law Review*, 59 (5) (1996), pp. 675–94.

32 Fehlberg, *Sexually Transmitted Debt*.

33 J. C. W. Wylie, 'An Irish Perspective on Protecting a Non-Owning Spouse in the Home', in F. Meisel and P. Cook (eds), *Property and Protection: Legal Rights and Restrictions* (Oxford: Hart Publishing, 2000).

34 In England and Wales, the interests of banks in realizing their securities were for many years given priority over the need to protect occupiers of mortgaged property. See Thomson, 'Monied Might or Social Justice?'.

35 I. Ovonji-Odida, F. Muhereza, L. Eturu and L. Alden Wily, *Impact of Spousal Co-ownership of the Primary Household Property: A Short Study Conducted for the Land Act Implementation Project* (Kampala: Ministry of Water, Lands and Environment, 2000).

36 This is a common response to attempts to constrain lending by commercial banks. In Britain, for example, the Law Commission has tended to avoid any measure which would increase the risks to which commercial lenders are exposed. See Law Commission, *Transfer of Land: Land Mortgages*, Report No. 204 (1991).

7 Conclusion

This book has been concerned with a central aspect of the recent revival of law and development, that is, land reform. Seeking to explain why law has come to prominence at this time as a solution to the problems of land, it has explored the politics of land reform and has studied, for the first time, the main actors in this important process. In exploring the different levels at which land law reform is being promoted, this book has drawn attention to 'the tight fit'[1] between international financial institutions, African governments, technical legal consultants and civil society groups. While the last two decades of land reform in Africa have alerted us to the continued importance of studying the role of the state which for Marx 'begat' the conditions for capitalist production 'hothouse-fashion', the emergence of 'regimes of ... globalised management'[2] have demanded simultaneous attention to the role of multilateral institutions in land law reform.

In drawing attention to how a network of African land law reform has been created and sustained in the last two decades, I have sought to represent its workings at both the international level and at the level of the nation-state for, as Ahmad has argued, it is necessary to pay attention both to globalized supervision and to the globalized state: 'To the extent that relatively similar processes are duplicated in a number of countries under regimes of both nation-state and globalised management (the World Bank, the WTO, etc.), in a system that is itself transnational, a supervening authority above national and local authorities is again an objective requirement of the system as a whole.'[3]

While the focus of this book has been on the creation of a network of land law reform and the possibilities of its endurance over time, it is also important to be alert to the contingency of networks, to their 'fragile efficacy',[4] and to the possibilities of their falling into disuse. I argued in Chapter 1 that by the late 1960s we had witnessed the abandonment of the original network of law and development and that what has occurred since has been its subsequent revival with land law reform as a central element. Far from being of merely descriptive interest, I would suggest that this potential for networks to fall into disrepair has important implications for political intervention. The task of identifying the nature, extent and location of a network's fragility may be the first step in developing strategies to challenge its dominance. Panitch and Gindin have reminded us that 'a global capitalist order is always a contingent social construct: the actual development and continuity of such an order must be problematised'.[5] Imagining the possibilities for the development of a progressive politics that challenges the project for the privatization of land requires us to heed the contingency of the contemporary network of land law reform. This can be done by elaborating, as I have done here, on its construction and maintenance, while also attending to the likelihood and prospects of its continuity. If, as Kennedy has argued, debate about distributional choices is silenced by the contemporary adherence to the rule of law as a development strategy, the question remains how might law and development be recaptured as 'a broad vocabulary of struggle'[6] for it is clear that 'Hatukushirikishwa' ('We did not participate) remains the 'battle-cry of the people' today just as it was when they gave evidence to the Shivji Commission in 1991.[7]

While there appears to have been increased attention paid to issues of poverty reduction in recent years, the prominence of poverty reduction in international development discourse[8] should not be allowed to mask the fact that, at a conceptual level, understandings of poverty remain undeveloped.[9] The simplistic approach that has been adopted to date is encapsulated in the judgment of Alan Budd, the former chief economic adviser to the

British Treasury, when he declared that '[w]hat Hernando de Soto has done is to solve the mystery of poverty'.[10]

As Polanyi has shown, governments must on occasion intervene violently to create market freedom.[11] The administration of economic 'shock therapy' to Iraq – the sale of state assets, the elimination of ownership restrictions, the opening up of borders[12] – reminds us that laissez-faire is always and everywhere planned. If the Pentagon has been charged with playing the 'global slumlord'[13] of the third world city, other partners in Washington's institutional complex are evidently directing their attention to the rural third world. The policy directive emanating from the World Bank that I have explored in this book indicates that, for it, land that is not mapped and registered is seen as remaining dangerously outside the rule of law. I have already suggested that the World Bank's plans for third world agriculture – which emphasize the desirability, to say nothing of inevitability, of individual tenure and which insist that the label 'law' should be confined to the law of the state – stand in marked contrast to the everyday reality of a ubiquitous legal pluralism in which the terrain of the global south is characterized by communal land tenure and adherence to non-state law. In what follows, I would like to move beyond this analysis to suggest briefly that key policy documents emanating from the World Bank and key international aid donors seek in fact to organize this terrain and to give form to economic and social relations.

If we fail to formalize land relations, we are told, we condemn land to the status of dead capital. Land that is allowed to be used only for subsistence is a dead asset which holds back economic development. By releasing such dead capital, we will liberate peasant farmers into a global marketplace in which their sole productive asset, their land, can be used as collateral for loans. In the World Bank's 'operation freedom', this integration of the south's farmers into the global commodity market will bring them choice: between basic subsistence and intensive market

Conclusion

139

productions, between dependence on exclusively peasant economic and social relations and petty bourgeois entrepreneurship. There is familiar resignation that some collateral damage may occur: integrated into an unstable, fluctuating world economy, and sometimes unable to keep the market at bay, some indebted farms will be lost.

If the present project for the formalization of land tenure conceives of the terrain of the third world as parcelized, individualized and registered, this approach may be contrasted with the topology of the African colonial and early postcolonial state. British colonialism in Africa furnished us with the concept of trust land but the topology of the early postcolonial state was different. The way in which it conceived of and sought to reorganize the space of the state placed an emphasis on collective development. The space of the state was held in common. The state, not the individual, borrowed on the international debt market. In this way, a joint debt burden was carried by all citizens. Uniquely, the timeline for the repayment of this collective debt was also shared.

The debt crisis of the early 1980s and the subsequent intervention of the International Monetary Fund marked the end of history for this developmental project. The devaluation of the state as an agent of development opened the way for a restructuring of the state. International financial institutions could now define a new topology in the form of parcelized, individualized landholding. In contrast to the early postcolonial state's collective time horizon, the debt burden is instead now experienced individually. The project to formalize land orients each individual landholder towards some future discharge of a debt burden acquired when previously subsistence land is used as collateral for loans.

As dispossession follows hard on the heels of rural debt, capitalist agricultural arrangements will find at their disposal an increasingly landless proletarianized rural workforce.[14] The future time of the indebted small farmer will come to be replaced by the new time horizon of agrarian business corporations which, as Bakan has recently demonstrated, have 'through a bizarre legal alchemy' been transformed into persons with their own identity.[15] Corporations in the agrarian context will inscribe a new, as yet unknown, topology on the terrain of the third world.

Current thinking on the formalization of land relations holds that the terrain of the global south is to be characterized by full, private property rights exercised over discrete and delineated landholdings. Plans for the transformation of rural life operate 'through the trope of individuality'.[16] A new language has to be learned: the language of private property, payoffs and productivity, and of efficiency, exchange and incentives. In this triumphalist vision of economic rationality, a 'disembodied homo economicus'[17] will sweep aside solidaristic social relations and practices of subsistence.

Feminist economics has recently begun to critique the assumption of the ubiquity of what it has named variously as the 'Robinson Crusoe'[18] or the 'Davos man'[19] model of economic rationality, pointing out that norms associated with the market do not apply to the sphere of unpaid work in which goods and services are perceived as being produced for use rather than for exchange. As I suggested in Chapter 6, international financial institutions' clear-sightedness about capital has not been matched by their insights into labour. On the contrary, there seems to be a continuing presumption in much international development discourse of the coercive power of the male head of the household and the need for feudal family relations and patriarchal kinship structures. On the neo-liberal landscape of the global south then, indebted, rational economic man oriented towards the future time of the market is taken to be accompanied by altruistic woman whose orientation is only towards clear and present labour.

A concerted 'assault on peasant cultures'[20] will mark the coming years. As I have shown, the creation and endurance of a

Conclusion

network of land law reform, linking the local and the global in important new ways, has served to place the formalization of land relations at the centre of the new law and development.

Notes

1 A. Ahmad, 'Imperialism of Our Time', in L. Panitch and C. Leys (eds), *Socialist Register 2004: The New Imperial Challenge* (London: Merlin Press, 2004), pp. 43–62, 46.

2 Ibid., pp. 45–6.

3 Ibid.

4 B. Latour, 'Give Me a Laboratory and I Will Raise the World', in K. D. Knorr-Cetina and M. Mulkay (eds), *Science Observed: Perspectives in the Social Study of Science* (London: Sage, 1983), p. 166.

5 L. Panitch and S. Gindin, 'Global Capitalism and American Empire', in Panitch and Leys (eds), *Socialist Register 2004*, pp. 1–42.

6 D. Kennedy, 'Laws and Developments', in A. Perry and J. Hatchard (eds), *Law and Development: Facing Complexity in the 21st Century* (London: Cavendish, 2003), p. 17.

7 I. G. Shivji, 'Contradictory Perspectives on Rights and Justice in the Context of Land Tenure Reform in Tanzania', Paper presented to a meeting of the Academic Staff Council, University of Dar es Salaam, 1997.

8 P. Cammack, 'What the World Bank Means by Poverty Reduction and Why It Matters', in *New Political Economy*, 9 (2) (2004), pp. 189–211.

9 For a detailed critique, see P. Cammack, 'Making Poverty Work', in L. Panitch and C. Leys (eds), *Socialist Register 2002: A World of Contradictions* (London: Merlin Press, 2001), pp. 193–210.

10 See <www.ild.org.pe/home.htm> (accessed December 2005).

11 K. Polanyi, *The Great Transformation* (Boston: Beacon Press, 1957).

12 N. Klein, 'Baghdad Year Zero', *Harper's Magazine*, September 2004, pp. 43–53.

13 M. Davis, 'The Pentagon as Global Slumlord', *Socialist Review*, May 2004, p. 16.

14 For an instructive account of the crisis of agriculture experienced by the United States in the 1980s, see K. M. Dudley, *Debt and Dispossession: Farm Loss in America's Heartland* (Chicago: University of Chicago Press, 2000).

15 J. Bakan, *The Corporation: The Pathological Pursuit of Profit and Power* (London: Constable and Robinson, 2004), p. 16.

16 R. Patel and P. McMichael, 'Third Worldism and the Lineages of

Global Fascism: The Regrouping of the Global South in the Neo-Liberal Era', *Third World Quarterly*, 25 (1) (2004), pp. 231–54, 240.

17 U. Grapard, 'Robinson Crusoe: The Quintessential Economic Man?', *Feminist Economics*, 1 (1) (1995), pp. 33–52.

18 Ibid.

19 L. Beneria, 'Globalization, Gender and the Davos Man', *Feminist Economics*, 5 (3) (1999), pp. 61–83.

20 Patel and McMichael, 'Third Worldism and the Lineages of Global Fascism', p. 235.

Conclusion

Index

Agarwal, B., 99
agency, in land reform project, 82–9
agrarian reform, new wave, 67
alienation of land, 42, 46
Amin, Samir, 9
anthrax, vaccination against, 13–14
anthropology, discrediting of, 14

Bank of Uganda, Agricultural Secretariat, 71
Bankers' Association of Uganda, 113; lobbying against, 132
banks: involvement in land law reform, 122; role in land relations, 111
von Benda-Beckmann, F., 19
Bernstein, H., 32–3, 116, 118
Blair, Tony, 62; 'Commission for Africa', 62–3, 64, 65
Brazil, 38
British colonialism, 42
Budd, Alan, 138–9
Byres, T.J., 31–9

cadastral systems, modernization of, 33
Callinicos, Alex, 9
capitalism, as contingent social construct, 138
civil society, definition of, 6
civil society groups, ambiguous role of, 23
Clinton, Bill, endorsement of de Soto, 2, 3
Coldham, Simon, 88

collateral, land as see land, as collateral
commercial lenders, role of, 129–32
Commission for a Strong and Prosperous Africa, 32, 62–3
Commission of Inquiry into the Land Law System (Njonjo Commission) (Kenya), 42
commissions of inquiry, 22, 43–5
commons: dependence of poor on, 41; new tragedy of, 40–1
concentration of land ownership, 39, 40, 42
consent, 113, 131; as juridical concept, centrality of, 112
Convention for the Elimination of Discrimination against Women (CEDAW), 104, 108, 117
corporations, assume personal identity, 141
Côte d'Ivoire, 41
credit, formal, promotion of, 24, 114
credit markets, rural, 52, 127; consequences of, for women, 122; creation of, 7, 8, 24; promotion of, 58, 59, 62, 122, 124, 129
customary tenure see tenure
Cutler, A.C., 17–19, 67, 68–70

Davis, M., 21
debt: crisis of 1980s, 140; experienced individually, 140; of rural inhabitants, 61

Department for International
Development (DfID), 1, 4,
5, 32, 45, 56, 62, 71, 72, 87,
108–9, 128
developmentalism, 9, 34
discretionary powers: limiting
of, 91, 94, 95; problem of, 89;
replacement of, 90
divorce, in Uganda, 106
donors, 51–77; role of, 62–5

East African Women's
Conference (1993), 101
The Economist, 7–8
elites, role of, 70
enclosure, 41
enterprise zones, creation of, 40
exit, practice of, 21

family labour, 124–6; availability
of, 59; of women, 37; unpaid,
60
family land, alienation of,
109–10
financializing of land relations,
23
flexibility of labour, 60
food insecurity, 39
foreclosure, 72
forests, conservation of, 40
Foundation for Building the
Capital of the Poor, 4

gender, and tenure reform,
101–5
gender issues, 37, 117;
marginalization of, 105
gender progressive groups: in
contesting law, 99–121; in
East Africa, 100–14
gender relations, worsening of,
24, 122, 124–9
geographical space, collapsing
of, 87

Gesellschaft für technische
Zusammenarbeit (GTZ), 5,
56, 62
Ghana, 2; company law drafted,
14, 94
GKI (Griffin, Khan, Ickowitz)
thesis, 36–9
globalization, 17, 34, 117;
importance of law within, 18;
of law, 17, 18
good governance, 99; donors'
interest in, 81
Gower, L.C.B., 14, 94
Griffin, Keith, 36–9

household, problematization
of, 126
housework, payment for, 125
Houtzager, P., 115–16

Ickowitz, Amy, 36–9
illiteracy, legal, 130
implementation, problems of,
123–4
India, land market in, 57
individuality, trope of, 141
Institute for Liberty and
Democracy, 3
intensive cultivation, 37
International Institute
for Environment and
Development (IIED), 62
International Monetary Fund
(IMF), 140
internet: consultations over
land reform, 44; over-reliance
on, by World Bank, 5
investment, foreign, 72;
encouragement of, 95

judiciary, role of, 129–32

Kennedy, David, 11–12, 19, 67
Kenya, 42

Movimiento Rural Sem Terra
(MST) (Brazil), 38, 115–16,
118
Moyo, Sam, 39, 41, 114–15
Mulgan, Geoff, 62

Natural Resources Institute
(University of Greenwich), 62
neo-liberalism, 17, 19, 67, 68;
consequences of, 127
network theory, 14, 18, 46, 70
networks, 83; contingency of,
138
networks of land reform, 16, 23,
65, 80, 82–9, 100, 137; global,
69–72
non-governmental
organizations (NGOs), in
land reform, growth of, 110

occupation of land, tactic of, 38,
41, 114, 116
owner-operated farms, 59–60;
efficiency of, 124–6

Pasteur, Louis, laboratory of,
13–14, 83, 84
paying for law, 51–77
peasant cultures: assault on,
141; male elites in, 69
Peters, P., 40
Polanyi, K., 139
poverty, reduction of, 2, 4, 8, 38,
58, 59, 61, 63, 112, 126, 138
Powell, Colin, 11
private sphere, domination in,
125
privatization, 127; of land, 23,
54–61, 87
property: as consensus on use
of assets, 12; definition of,
11–12
property rights, formalization
of, 2, 9, 32

redistributive land reform, 34,
35–6, 37
Royal Africa Institute, 62
rule of law, 15, 99, 139; as
development strategy, 12,
83, 138; as first cousin to
capital, 53; as focus of aid
projects, 11; elements of, 10;
promotion of, 52–3
'rule of law aid', 52
rural movements: ideologies
and tactics of, 114–16; in
contesting law, 99–121;
relation to state law, 115, 118

science, sociology of, 13, 14, 16,
23, 78, 80, 83–7
Shihata, Ibrahim, 10
Shivji, Issa, 44–6, 69, 90–1
Shivji Commission, 68, 106, 138;
Report of, 91
SOAS school of agrarian studies,
36
de Soto, Hernando, 2–4, 8,
11–12, 19–21, 63, 64, 81, 89,
139; *The Mystery of Capital …*;
2–3; visit to UK, 62
de Sousa Santos, B., 10
South Africa, land reform in, 89
spousal co-ownership, in
Uganda, 105–14; lobbying
against, 132
squatting *see* occupation of land
state, devalued as agent of
development, 140
surety wives, cases involving,
128

Tanzania, 15, 23, 100–14;
draft land bill, 103, 105;
Land Act (1998), 44, 46,
66, 68, 72, 90, 105, 130;
land reform in, 44, 51, 89,
90; National Commission

promotion of rural credit markets, 59; role of, 4–9, 22 (in privatization of public goods, 127)

World Trade Organization (WTO), 2, 137

Yeros, P., 114–15

www.ingramcontent.com/pod-product-compliance
Lightning Source LLC
Chambersburg PA
CBHW022322280326
41932CB00010B/1199